Contents

KT-442-675

About the authors

This eleventh edition of *Decisions at 13/14+* has been produced by the team of authors responsible for the widely used *CLIPS* series of careers information leaflets, *KeyCLIPs* and *eCLIPS*.

Jenny Barron, Tamsin Foxwell and Debbie Steel have also written, revised and edited other careers and educational guides. Between them, they have broad and varied experience of the worlds of education, employment and careers advice.

CRAC: the Career Development Organisation, an educational charity based in Cambridge established in 1964.

CRAC's goals are:

- to promote the importance of career development and career-related learning, for the benefit of individuals, the community and the economy

- to influence individuals' attitudes and motivations towards career development and learning to enable them to make wise decisions and optimal use of their talents and skills

- to encourage the structured growth of active and conscious career development, and to promote best practice amongst educational institutions, employers and individuals.

To achieve these, CRAC:

- undertakes research into the needs of individuals and employers in respect of career development

- devises and delivers learning programmes for young people at school and throughout higher education

- works at the education/business interface in partnership with employers, careers practitioners and educational establishments

- provides specialist knowledge and consultancy for organisations in the field of career development.

For information on any of our activities, or to contact us, visit www.crac.org.uk

Part one
Looking forward

Chapter one

Making a start

If you are 13 or over and you are about to choose your subjects for the next school year, this book is for you. Year 9 is the time to look ahead and to start finding out more about life beyond school. *Decisions at 13/14+* will help you decide which subjects and courses to take and to start thinking about your various options for the future. Although you don't need to decide which career you want just yet, it helps to start giving it some thought. Don't forget, you can always change your mind later!

The book includes:

- how to go about making decisions
- information on the various qualifications available

- advice on choosing your subjects
- options after 16
- a list of careers, what they involve and their main entry requirements
- how you can find out more.

The book will also help you find answers to these important questions:

- what are my strengths?
- what areas do I need to work on?
- what skills do I want to develop further?
- which subjects must I take?
- which subjects should I choose?
- what will I learn in each subject?
- how will I be assessed?
- how will my choices affect my career prospects?
- how do I go about making my choice?

Getting to know yourself

In order to work out which school subjects are right for you, you need to know what kind of person you are.

In school...

Consider which subjects you enjoy and which subjects you are best at. Use the following list to help you think about what things you like doing at school:

- project work
- working with numbers
- writing essays and assignments
- laboratory work
- learning languages
- using computers
- designing and drawing

- playing sports
- performing e.g. in plays or concerts
- making things
- working with others
- meeting deadlines
- anything else...?

In your spare time...

When you are not in school, how do you spend your spare time? Use the following list to help you think about what things you enjoy doing:

- reading
- playing sports or exercising
- writing
- playing computer games or using the internet
- building or repairing things
- acting, singing, dancing or playing musical instruments
- designing and making things
- budgeting your money
- going out with friends or attending youth clubs etc
- organising things, e.g. parties or trips
- being outdoors whatever the weather
- anything else...?

What type of person are you?

Now you have thought a little more about what you enjoy doing at school and in your spare time, you may have more of an idea about what subjects would be best for you. For instance, if you are:

- creative, you will like subjects that give you the opportunity to design things and improve your artistic talents
- good with words, you may enjoy subjects where there is a lot of written work

- confident when talking with others, subjects with oral work, such as languages, will suit you

- good with computers, find out what subjects will give you the chance to use ICT in your studies

- sporty, you may be able to take physical education for GCSE

- good with figures, science and maths-based subjects will probably suit you

- practical, find out which subjects will give you a chance to do plenty of 'hands-on' work

- a sociable-type of person, you will enjoy subjects where you have a chance to work with others in a team

- good at organising and meeting deadlines, courses that include project work will suit you.

Now use the rest of this book to help you with your decisions.

Chapter two

Making connections

It's a whole new world out there ...

We all know about school – sitting in class, listening to the teacher, churning out homework, with the same timetable week after week, day after day!

The world of work appears to be very different from school – interesting activities, meeting lots of people, having more freedom, and getting paid! It sounds an attractive alternative to school, with not a glimmer of homework on the horizon.

But is it so different?

In fact, school and work are more closely connected than you may think. Take a look at the High Street in Anytown, UK, and see what is going on.

The following high-street businesses are all illustrated in the drawing on the previous page:

- a bank
- a fashion shop
- a travel agents
- an insurance company
- a chemists
- a fitness club.

Think about

- What do people working in these businesses actually do every day?
- What skills and knowledge do they use?
- Which school subjects will have helped them gain the necessary skills and knowledge?

The following table gives you an idea of the type of work you might do in each business. In the second column we've suggested a few school subjects that might be helpful to do that work. Can you make the connection?

Typical business activities	Useful school subjects
Bank • Keeping customers' accounts according to their wishes • Lending and investing money • Advising people how to run their businesses	Maths Business studies English
Fashion shop • Knowing which clothes people want to buy • Ordering them from the manufacturer • Thinking up artistic window displays	Art and design Economics Home economics: textiles

Typical business activities	Useful school subjects
Travel agents • Planning trips for customers • Dealing with travellers' cheques and foreign currencies • Checking bookings with overseas hotels and travel companies	Geography Modern foreign languages Leisure and tourism Maths
Insurance company • Meeting members of the public • Working out how much customers have to pay to insure themselves against accidents • Writing letters to customers	English Maths ICT
Chemists • Dispensing drugs according to doctors' prescriptions • Selling other medicines across the counter • Giving advice when needed	Science/chemistry English Maths
Fitness club • Publicising activities • Instructing exercise classes • Scheduling rotas	Business studies PE Art and design Design and technology

Maybe you thought of other subjects that would also be useful. Did you notice that some of the same skills would be useful for many of the different business activities?

The skills connection

The practical skills of communication, application of number, ICT, improving your own learning and performance, working with others, and problem solving are the skills needed in almost any job.

You can gain key skills qualifications in these subjects as they form part of, or can be taken alongside, many of the courses and training that you will do in year 10 and beyond. From 2010 in England, functional skills will replace the main key skills qualifications in English, maths and ICT.

Your school subjects will help you develop these and other skills that will be useful in the world of work.

Think about the following subjects, for example.

- Drama involves developing trust and understanding of the people you are working with.

- In geography, you may be asked to work in a group. You need to be able to listen to others, discuss their ideas, and come to an agreement on what you will all do.

- For business studies, you may have to set up a mock company, where a board of directors or a product development team has to work together – just like in a real business situation.

You will be developing your skills in 'working with others' in all of these situations.

Work-related learning

At Key Stage 4 you have the opportunity to study courses designed to help you make a very direct connection between school and work. Diplomas, Young Apprenticeships and some GCSE courses, for example, aim to give you an insight into different areas of work, and help you gain some relevant skills.

GCSE courses in subjects such as applied business, engineering, health and social care, for example, investigate broad areas of work through assignments and often include some work experience.

Diploma subjects include construction and the built environment, creative and media, engineering, information technology, and society, health and development. A total of 17 subjects will be available by 2011. Diplomas mix learning at school with work experience, project work, and the chance to gain hands-on, practical skills maybe in a college or workplace.

Your school may offer you the opportunity to do other courses to help you gain specialist or general work-related skills leading to NVQ, BTEC or OCR National qualifications, for example. Ask your teachers for more information.

Young Apprenticeships allow you to focus on an area of work that you are particularly interested in and spend some time each week on work experience.

Some other skills developed through school subjects

Researching and analysing information – most subjects involve this skill, especially sciences, business studies, social sciences, geography, history, citizenship and economics.

Thinking creatively – art and design, music, drama, design and technology, creative and media are the obvious examples, but you can also think creatively in the sciences, engineering and manufacturing, and in any subject that involves solving problems.

Observing – many subjects involve good observation skills. For example, visual observation is needed for art and design, or design and technology. While observation of people and behaviour is used for creative writing in English or for social sciences, religious studies, and society, health and development.

Measuring – you need to measure accurately for design and technology, art and design, engineering, science, and construction and the built environment.

Selecting materials – the right materials can make all the difference in art and design, design and technology and home economics.

Setting up experiments and drawing conclusions from them – again, science is the obvious subject, but you may also develop these skills in engineering and ICT. Some activities in social sciences and business studies can involve experimentation of a different kind.

Caring for the environment and for living things – your school may offer environmental and land-based studies, otherwise geography, health and social care, and science/biology are the most likely subjects.

Understanding yourself and others – social sciences, citizenship, PE, drama, geography and history all offer chances to learn about individuals and society. Studying a modern foreign language also involves learning about different cultures.

Using a language other than English – modern foreign languages are the most obvious, but you may also come across subjects like Latin and classical Greek, and other languages in music, art and design, leisure and tourism and ICT.

Developing theories – social science, history, geography, sciences, engineering and economics all give you the opportunity to work out whether certain events can be predicted in advance.

Performing – music, drama, dance and PE will all develop your performance skills.

Working independently – all subjects should give you the chance to prove that you can work on your own initiative to some extent.

You may want to refer back to this list when you come to making your final choice of courses and subjects. Both academic and work-related subjects can provide many opportunities to build on and develop a range of work and life skills. You can probably think of other examples yourself.

You could choose to study in the areas where you are most skilled already. Alternatively, you could deliberately choose subjects that will develop skills in areas where there's room for improvement.

And outside the classroom?

Don't think the only time you are acquiring skills is during formal learning. The skills you gain through your hobbies and interests can be just as important.

If you play sport in or out of school, you will be developing your teamwork skills and your communication skills, as well as improving things like agility, fitness and balance. If you are called upon to referee or judge then you are analysing and making decisions. If you are team captain you are developing leadership skills – and possibly problem solving too!

Leadership, organisational and budgeting skills can be developed through helping to run any club or group you are involved in. Saturday and holiday jobs – as well as work experience through your school –

depending on exactly what you do, will help to improve your business understanding, numeracy, communication skills, time-management, negotiating, forward planning, teamwork skills etc.

Take a moment to think about your out-of-school activities and the skills you are developing through them. Can you make a connection between these skills and any school subjects? How about any jobs that may use these skills?

Things people say

By all means have a point of view, but it is too early to make final career decisions like this.

Reasons for keeping an open mind

- There are many more career options available to you than you will be aware of at this stage of your life. You could be missing out on exciting possibilities that you have not even heard of yet!

- You will develop and change as a person over the next few years. You will learn new skills and discover new qualities within yourself. These may make other career options more appealing to you.

While it may be too early to have definite plans for a career, you do still have to make your subject choices this year. Here are some guidelines to help you.

- Aim for a subject choice that leaves your future plans flexible.

- If you have a broad idea of a career, make sure you know any subject requirements.

- Over the next few years, take all the opportunities you can to find out more about different careers.

We will look at how to go about this in the remainder of this book.

Chapter three

Making the move

No-one stays on at school for ever! At some point in the future you will be applying for your first job as your life moves on.

Finding a job that you enjoy and that gives you good prospects for the future will be dependant on many different factors. Some things you *can't* control – which jobs are available, where they are based, how much competition you will have when you apply, and so on. But some of the things you *can* control – starting with the choices you make now – will make a big difference to how your life unfolds.

Here are your goals for the next few years.

Choose your subjects

This book will help you make the right choices for you. The National Curriculum makes some subjects compulsory, but there is still plenty of room for choice. Chapter five looks in detail at what you will study, and at how you can best combine different subjects and types of courses.

Find out about careers

There is almost no limit to the sources that will give you up-to-date information. Chapter ten of this book directs you to many. Make sure you try the software packages and websites that are available for careers guidance.

Get to know yourself

Your school may also be using a computer program to help you identify your interests and think about your personality. Take this seriously and discuss the results with your careers coordinator/teacher, your personal/ careers adviser and your parents.

Make the most of your work experience

During year 10 or 11, you will have the opportunity for work experience. This may be your first taste of what the world of work is really like. You will spend one or two weeks with a local employer, who will give you the chance to try out a job or range of jobs. There may be limits as to what is available, but, in general, you will have the choice of where you wish to spend your work experience time.

You may have the opportunity to study closely what one particular person does in their job – that's called 'work shadowing'.

Take this opportunity to ask all sorts of questions, and look keen. You'll find that employers and employees will be more helpful if you show an interest in what they are doing. You may be given materials to help you prepare for work experience and to keep details of your placement in the form of a daily log.

Through work experience, you'll learn more about yourself too – your likes and dislikes, and your abilities.

Achieve good grades

This is the most important goal. For example, four or five GCSEs at grades A*-C will give you an excellent foundation to go forward in almost any direction. English and maths are particularly desired by employers, and are a must for many further and higher education courses.

Achieving good grades will open all sorts of doors to you, and that means you have more choice in the way your life and career develop.

Beyond 16

There are also some important choices beyond 16 which you should be aware of even now. These are outlined briefly below, but more details can be found in chapter eight.

Further education

Staying on in full-time education is a way of increasing your future options even further. You can take advanced-level courses in sixth forms or at colleges, leading to AS and A levels, Advanced Diplomas and other qualifications. These courses can lead into either a job or higher education.

Work-based learning

If you know what kind of work you want to do, and would like to start learning in a practical way in the workplace when you reach 16, then work-based learning may be for you. You would be based with an employer and also spend part of your time at a training centre or college. Apprenticeships are an example of work-based learning. These are available in a wide range of careers, and lead to National Vocational Qualifications (NVQs) at levels 2 and 3.

If you decide to get a job, make sure that training is part of the deal or else you will find it hard to progress.

Higher education

If you are already sure about your chosen career, you should check now whether it requires a higher education qualification, such as a degree. If it does, that may affect the subjects you need to choose now. Even if you have no specific career plan in mind, getting well-qualified is, and always will be, the door that opens up the most opportunities.

The books, resources and websites listed in chapter ten will show you what is on offer and where you can study.

Learning for life

Who knows what the job scene will be like when you finish full-time education and training? Jobs are changing all the time, and they are no longer 'for life'. Nowadays, most people change jobs, and perhaps careers, several times during their working lives. Changing jobs is made easier if you keep up to date with new technology and new ways of working.

So, it is important to keep learning – gaining new qualifications and skills throughout your career. This is referred to as 'lifelong learning'. Employees with the right skills will always be valued.

There are many different ways you can work, too. These include working on short-term contracts, doing temporary jobs, working part time and working from home. Being self-employed is an increasingly popular option. As working patterns become more flexible, so you have to be prepared to change with them and adapt to them.

Making the move

Getting qualified, choosing a career and starting your first job will not happen overnight. It is a gradual process and will involve a number of decisions. You need to take each step with thought and care, and get all the advice available.

Many of the decisions will follow on logically from decisions you have made earlier. There are always fresh chances if things go wrong, but it will be better to get it right first time!

Those who went before you in 2006

Take a look at the results of a survey of pupils who finished year 11 in 2006 – 59% achieved five or more GCSEs at grades A*-C.

Of that year group, around:

78% stayed in full-time education at the end of year 11

6% went into government-supported training, e.g. Apprenticeships

6% went into other employment

7% were not in education, employment or training

4% went into other education or training.

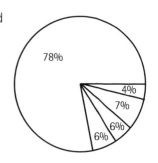

Chapter four

Making decisions

There are so many varied subjects and courses out there that there is not enough time between now and 16 to take them all. This may be the first time you have been asked to make a decision that will affect your future. That may sound overwhelming, but you'll have lots of help.

"Am I the indecisive type? Yes. I mean, No. Er, that is to say ... maybe ... "

How easy do you find it to make decisions?

To make a start, try some decision-making now!

Which of the following do you prefer?

You choose	
For lunch:	vegetable soup **or** burger and chips?
Tonight on TV:	EastEnders **or** Coronation Street?
Saturday night:	romantic movie **or** youth club?

Now try these:

You choose	
Next holiday:	Bangkok **or** Guatemala?
For pudding:	mango sorbet **or** star fruit?
This weekend:	paragliding **or** ice hockey?

Making the decisions in the first set was probably easy, but you may have found the second set more difficult. There is a simple reason for this. Those in the first set are easy because you are probably familiar with all of the options. If you have some experience of what is on offer, you can make decisions with confidence.

With the second set, you probably have not been to either place, tasted either pudding, or attempted either sport. To choose without experience may mean you have to work at the decision a little.

What's on the horizon?

The most obvious decision you are going to have to make shortly is which subjects you are going to take in years 10 and 11. But that is only one of several decisions that are on the horizon:

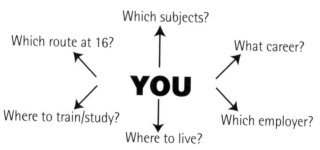

What can make these decisions seem hard is that they are all connected. The subjects you choose will affect the type of career you can follow. The job you get will affect where you decide to live. What you decide to do at 16 may affect where you train, and so on! It can seem daunting, but working out the answer to just one of these questions will help everything else fall into place.

Six logical steps to making a decision

Below is a series of steps which, if you take them slowly, get your facts straight and take plenty of advice, should help you come to a sensible decision. Remember, you are not searching for one right answer. You are looking for one possible answer among several.

1. Get the question clear

What are you being asked to decide?

Why are you being asked this?

2. Think about your goals

What is the most important thing you want to achieve?

Do you have any other goals?

How important are they?

3. Find out the facts

What are your options?

Where can you find out more about them?

4. Weigh them up

Do any of your options help you achieve your goals?

Are some options better than others at achieving your goals?

5. Make the decision

Which options let you achieve your most important goals?

Is one option starting to come out on top?

6. Check results

Does the decision look right?

Does the decision feel right?

If things change, how and when can you change your decision?

Putting it into practice

Here's an example of using the six steps to decide where to go on holiday.

1. Get the question clear

What are we trying to decide, and why?

- Where to go on holiday so that the whole family has a good time.

2. Think about your goals

Do we want:

- to stay in the UK or go abroad?

- self-catering or a hotel?

- a luxury holiday or somewhere cheap and cheerful?

- lots of activities laid on or to be left to relax?

We've decided we want to go abroad, and because we're on a budget, self-catering will be cheapest. We love to just take it easy – so we want somewhere we can relax.

3. Find out the facts

We've narrowed down our options to a villa in Spain or an apartment in Greece. To find out more about them, we're going to:

- get some holiday brochures from the travel agents

- buy a travel guide to find out more about each place

- ask our friends and neighbours, to hear what they recommend

- use the internet to read reviews of holidays in each area.

4. Weigh them up

When we compare both destinations against our goals:

- the villa in Spain sounds amazing, it's got its own pool and barbeque, but it is quite expensive

- the apartment in Greece is really close to the beach and there are lots of restaurants nearby.

5. Make the decision

It looks like we'd have a great time going to either Greece or Spain. But the most important thing on this occasion is how much it's all going to cost. So Greece it is!

6. Check results

How does our decision look and feel? And what if it doesn't work out?

- It makes good sense to go to Greece; it matches most of what we all want, including the price.
- We're all very excited about going to Greece – so it feels like a good decision.
- If it's not as good as we hope we'll go to Spain next year!

Which subjects shall I choose?

Apply the formula as before.

1. Get the question clear

What am I trying to decide, and why?

- I need to choose my options for year 10, and that includes subjects and types of courses.
- The choices I make now will take my life in a particular direction – I need to be sure it's the way I want to go!

2. Think about your goals

What do I want to achieve and what is most important to me?

- To get a particular job or to keep my options open?
- To develop my best skills and abilities or to learn new ones?
- To earn lots of money or to find satisfaction in other ways?
- To get out into the 'real world' as soon as possible or to continue my education for a few years yet?
- Something else entirely?

3. Find out the facts

What are my options and where can I find out more?

- Which subjects and courses does my school offer?

- Do I have access to any other courses run at local schools or colleges?

- What information can my school provide?

- When is my school's options event?

- Have I spoken to my personal adviser/careers coordinator?

- Have I used the rest of this book for information about subjects, courses and careers?

- Have I looked into some of the other resources available to me, such as those listed in chapter ten?

4. Weigh them up

When I compare my options against the things I want to achieve:

- which subjects and courses help me achieve my goals?

- which options help me achieve my most important goals?

5. Make the decision

Maybe one option stands out from all the rest – that makes life easy! Or maybe several options fit the bill – time to think really carefully about what is important to me.

6. Check results

Have I made a good choice? What if I haven't?

- Do I feel positive about what lies ahead? (Feeling a bit nervous is OK too – but dreading what comes next is a warning sign that you should act on).

- Have I checked with someone in the know that my choice makes sense – a teacher, personal adviser/careers coordinator, my parents etc?

- If, after I've given my courses a fair trial, I'm not happy with my decision, I'll get advice and find out what I can change. I won't leave it too long though, as that may make it harder to move on to something new.

Part two
It's your choice

Chapter five

The right mix

In years 10 and 11 (Key Stage 4), you will continue with certain subjects, but you'll be able to choose others. The National Curriculum helps you to keep your choice of subjects balanced. That way you will end up with a broad base of knowledge, understanding and skills which will stand you in good stead, whatever you do in the future.

It's exciting having some choice, but it's important to get the right mix of subjects for **you** and what you want to do in the future. It's impossible for **all** schools to offer **all** subjects, so whether you want to do art or Urdu, find out what's available.

This chapter examines the National Curriculum – the subjects you have to do and others you can choose. It'll also introduce you to GCSEs and other programmes you may be able to take.

The National Curriculum

There are subjects that are so important to our lives today that you have to study them. Other subjects you can choose because you are interested in them and/or because you know they will be important for a career you have in mind. The curriculums in England, Wales and Northern Ireland are broadly similar; information on England and Wales is provided below. For details on the **Northern Ireland Curriculum**, see: www.nicurriculum.org.uk

The curriculum in England

At Key Stage 4, all students must study:

- English
- maths
- science
- information and communication technology (ICT)
- physical education
- citizenship.

The first three subjects in the above list are normally taken as qualifications. ICT isn't a compulsory exam subject. In addition to the subjects listed above, you must also be taught religious education, sex education, careers education and work-related learning.

There are also non-statutory programmes of study for religious education, personal wellbeing (which includes sex, relationships and drugs education) and economic wellbeing and financial capability.

N.B. In some circumstances, your parent/carer can withdraw you from religious studies and the non-statutory aspects of sex education.

So, apart from the compulsory subjects, there are many different subjects you can choose from. Some schools make certain subjects compulsory; for instance, you may be expected to take a language or more than one science subject.

In addition to the compulsory subjects listed above, your choice of subjects **may** include:

- art and design
- business
- classical subjects, such as Latin or classical Greek
- construction and the built environment
- creative and media
- design and technology
- drama or performing/expressive arts
- engineering
- environmental and land-based studies
- geography
- hair and beauty studies
- health and social care/society, health and development
- history
- home economics
- hospitality
- leisure and tourism/travel and tourism/sport and leisure
- manufacturing
- media studies
- modern foreign languages, e.g. French, Spanish and German
- music
- public services
- retail
- social sciences.

Although not all of these subjects will be available, you have an **entitlement** to take a subject within each of the following areas:

- arts (art and design, music, dance, drama, media arts)
- design and technology

- humanities (geography, history)
- modern foreign languages.

You also have an entitlement to take at least two science GCSEs.

Changes to the National Curriculum are gradually being phased in, for instance:

- there will be clearer progression routes
- more emphasis on personalised learning programmes – with support for those who need it and greater challenge for others
- teaching of topics through a range of subjects (e.g. global warming could be taught through science and geography)
- schools will have the opportunity to build their own, local curriculum
- personal, learning and thinking skills, and functional skills (see page 42) will be taught through various programmes of study
- an entitlement for all young people to participate in positive activities which will develop their talents, including taking part in cultural activities both in and out of school.

Further information on the National Curriculum in England can be found on: http://curriculum.qca.org

The curriculum in Wales

The National Curriculum in Wales has recently been revised. It focuses on the learner, ensuring that vital skills (i.e. communication, ICT, number and thinking skills) are developed throughout the curriculum. The new curriculum also focuses on progression and provides greater flexibility.

All students in years 10 and 11 in Wales must take:

- English
- maths
- science
- Welsh
- physical education.

In addition, students have to learn about:

- personal and social education
- Wales, Europe and the world
- careers and the world of work.

In addition to compulsory studies, as in England, you have a wide range of subjects (and programmes) to choose from.

More information on the National Curriculum in Wales can be found on: http://wales.gov.uk/topics/educationandskills

Learning programmes: an overview

The National Curriculum allows you not only to choose some subjects, but also to mix and match different types of programmes to suit your needs. The following sections explain a little about the main types of programmes that may be available to you. Not all schools will be able to offer all of these; many now work with local colleges, other schools or work-based learning providers to broaden what they can offer.

If you live in England, you can get an idea of what types of programmes are available where you live through the 14-19 prospectuses. These can be found through: www.futures4me.co.uk

Entry level qualifications

Your teacher may advise you to take entry level programmes. Entry level certificates and awards are available in a wide range of National Curriculum subjects, basic skills and skills for working life. Entry level courses can be taken alongside GCSEs or may lead on to GCSE or other level 1 or 2 qualifications at a later stage. Entry level qualifications are assessed in various ways, e.g. through a portfolio of evidence, coursework and tests.

Foundation Learning Tier (FLT)

The FLT is a new term for programmes below level 2 taken by learners over the age of 14 in England. By 2010, new credit-based qualifications and units will be available. These will provide clear progression routes through entry and level 1 to level 2. A learner will have an initial assessment, a personalised learning programme tailored to their individual needs and undergo regular reviews. Programmes within the FLT will draw on the following areas:

- personal and social development
- vocational/subject-based learning
- basic skills and key/functional skills.

For more details on the FLT, see: www.qca.org.uk/flt

General Certificates of Secondary Education (GCSEs)

The majority of schools offer GCSEs as the main way of getting your qualifications at Key Stage 4. You will probably be expected to take GCSEs in English, maths and science. Most students take at least five GCSEs; in fact, it's usual to take seven or eight subjects.

Schools usually offer a wide range of subjects, some of which (e.g. health and social care, economics and psychology), you may not have studied before.

Chapter six describes GCSEs in more detail.

Short courses

In certain subjects, you may be given the opportunity to do a GCSE (short course) instead of a full GCSE. A GCSE (short course) is like a full GCSE but covers fewer topics, so only takes half the study time. The qualification counts as half a GCSE and can be taught over one or two years. GCSE (short courses) are available in a wide range of subjects, including:

- art and design
- business studies
- citizenship studies
- design and technology
- geography
- history
- ICT
- modern foreign languages
- physical education
- religious studies.

Applied GCSEs

An applied GCSE does not train you for a specific job, but gives you the knowledge, skills and understanding of a broad area of work. It can lead on to further study, training or employment. Applied GCSEs are usually taken as double awards (equivalent to two GCSEs), but single awards may be available in some subjects. Applied GCSEs include those in: applied art and design, applied business, engineering, health and social care, applied ICT, leisure and tourism, manufacturing and applied science.

International GCSEs (IGCSEs)

IGCSEs were originally designed for use overseas, but they are available at some independent schools and for private candidates as an alternative to GCSEs. Assessment is completely through exams; there's no coursework. IGCSEs are graded A*-C in the same way as GCSEs.

Diplomas

Available at some schools and colleges in England, these qualifications combine theoretical and practical learning. In years 10 and 11 they will be offered at two levels:

- **Foundation Diploma** – a level 1 qualification equivalent to five GCSEs at grades D-G

- **Higher Diploma** – a level 2 qualification equivalent to seven GCSEs at grades A*-C.

You learn about a broad area of employment and develop work-related skills, knowledge and understanding. You develop the functional skills of English, maths and ICT and also personal, learning and thinking skills. You can take options to specialise or to broaden your studies. GCSEs can be taken alongside a Diploma or included in the programme. A Higher Diploma can lead on to an Advanced Diploma, another further education course or a job with training.

See chapter seven for more detailed information about Diplomas and the subjects available.

Welsh Baccalaureate Qualification

The Welsh Baccalaureate is becoming widely available throughout Wales. It combines personal development skills with existing qualifications, such as GCSEs, to make one award. The Qualification provides the opportunity for a well-balanced curriculum and broad experiences. It can be taken in English, Welsh or a combination of the languages.

Students must complete a 'core programme' along with 'options' (i.e. a choice of academic or vocational subjects). There are no additional exams; assessment is based on the evidence collected during activities. The core programme is made up of:

- key skills (described later in this chapter)
- learning about Wales and its relationship with Europe and the rest of the world
- work-related education (involving work with an employer and participation in team enterprise activities)
- personal and social development (exploring issues, such as health, relationships and citizenship and includes an activity in the local community)
- an individual investigative project.

The Welsh Baccalaureate is available at three levels. In years 10 and 11, you may have the opportunity to take either the Foundation or Intermediate Diploma; the Advanced Diploma is a level 3 qualification.

- The **Foundation Diploma** comprises the Core Certificate at Foundation level, plus four GCSEs at grades D-G, an NVQ level 1 or a BTEC Introductory Diploma or equivalent. (At the time of writing, the Foundation Diploma is a pilot programme.)
- The **Intermediate Diploma** includes the Core Certificate at Intermediate level, plus four GCSEs at grades A*-C, an NVQ level 2 or a BTEC First Diploma or equivalent.

Work-related learning

If appropriate, in years 10 and 11, you may be able to follow a more practical, work-related programme in addition to taking the compulsory National Curriculum subjects. It may be possible for you to spend some time (e.g. one day a week) at a further education college, in a work-related learning placement, or on extended work experience, instead of at school. You could take work-related qualifications, possibly alongside GCSEs.

National Vocational Qualifications (NVQs)

If you undergo a work-related learning programme, you may have the opportunity to take an NVQ. NVQs offer training in a particular job area. They are assessed by observing your ability to do tasks at work and through a portfolio of work. More information about NVQs can be found in chapter eight.

Young Apprenticeships

Young Apprenticeships give you a taste of real work. If your school offers them, they may be available to you in areas such as health and social care, the motor industry and construction. You take the compulsory National Curriculum subjects at school, but spend 50 days over years 10 and 11 gaining experience with an employer, training provider or college.

You work towards an appropriate work-related qualification at level 2, such as an NVQ. Once you've completed your Young Apprenticeship, you could continue to a full Apprenticeship or take a related or unrelated course.

Vocationally Related Qualifications (VRQs)

Different awarding bodies offer a wide range of other qualifications which may be on offer to you in years 10 and 11. VRQs provide you with the skills and knowledge needed for a particular vocational area, such as hospitality or public services. VRQs may be short programmes of study or worth four or more GCSEs. They are usually assessed through coursework rather than exams. The VRQs available to you may include:

- BTEC Introductory qualifications (level 1) and BTEC First qualifications (at level 2 – roughly equivalent to four GCSEs at grades A*-C)

- OCR level 1 and 2 National qualifications

- certain City & Guilds qualifications.

Key skills and functional skills

It's essential to have certain practical skills in order to do well in your education, training, employment and in life in general.

Key skills are sometimes taken alongside other courses or work-related learning. They are assessed through a portfolio of evidence. For communication, application of number and ICT, there are also tests. The six key skills are:

- communication

- application of number

- ICT

- working with others

- problem solving

- improving your own learning and performance.

In England, **functional skills** will eventually replace the first three key skills listed above. English, maths and ICT are so important that these functional skills are becoming a critical part of many qualifications, including GCSEs in English, maths and ICT, Diplomas, Apprenticeships and the Foundation Learning Tier. Both key skills and functional skills can be achieved as qualifications in their own right. They are available at different levels (levels 1-4 for key skills, and entry level to level 2 for functional skills).

Things to consider

Where you have choices to make, try to make a well-balanced selection. Although a range of subjects is ideal, this may not always be appropriate. If you are already committed to a particular career choice, a limited concentration on one area of the curriculum could be helpful. Here are some typical questions you may ask yourself.

How many science subjects?

Depending on what is on offer at your school, you may be able to take:

- GCSE science (which covers all three science subjects) plus one or more GCSEs in additional science and/or separate science subjects

- GCSEs in all three sciences, i.e. biology, chemistry and physics

- GCSE applied science (double award).

As a minimum, most students take GCSE core science. Most students are expected to take more than one science GCSE, and this is essential for certain careers. Remember that if you take more than two science subjects at GCSE, a significant percentage of the week will be taken up, and this could upset your curriculum balance. However, if you have a career in mind for which science is important, then this could be the option for you. It's important to get advice from your teachers.

More than one creative arts subject?

Concentration on one area may also be sensible if you are particularly gifted in creative arts. For instance, music and drama are closely linked, and since becoming highly skilled requires continuous practice, there could be a good argument for keeping up more than one.

More than one language?

If you intend studying languages at university, or if you want to earn your living using them, consider taking at least two languages at GCSE.

Short course or full GCSE?

Don't view a GCSE (short course) as an easy option. The full GCSE should be studied if you have a specific career goal. However, you may find time to study a GCSE (short course) in order to broaden your education and develop transferable skills in ICT and/or a second foreign language, for example. GCSE (short courses) may also be a good option if you need extra time to take a formal qualification.

What about taking a work-related or vocational course?

You may think that you are a bit young to make a decision about your future career. That's fine because taking a broad range of subjects will keep most career options open. However, if you would like to find out about a broad area of work, or feel ready to spend some time on more practical tasks, some of programmes described earlier in this chapter, such as Diplomas, Young Apprenticeships and VRQs, may suit you.

Some people worry that doing a vocational qualification will reduce their options – this isn't necessarily true, but do seek advice.

Another way of gaining work experience is through a part-time job or by volunteering in your spare time. You will also do at least a week's work experience whilst in year 10 or 11.

Subject choice and your future career

In chapters six and seven, the main GCSE and Diploma subject areas are described. Although all subjects in the curriculum are important, to get into many courses and careers, you need good grades in English and maths. Also, sciences are a must for anyone who wants to enter scientific or engineering careers. Science is also important for many other jobs – from hairdressing to healthcare. Whereas subjects like business and social sciences are unlikely to be an essential entry requirement for careers, even in related fields, they may be valued by employers and course providers.

Don't choose subjects because you feel pressurised by other people. Also, don't pick a subject **only** because your friends are doing it, you think it will be an easy option or because you like the teacher. Other subjects may be far more important for what you are interested in doing in the future, or for keeping a wide range of careers open.

Your next step after GCSEs, or equivalent qualifications, may well be an advanced-level course, such as AS/A levels. If you already have certain subjects at that level in mind, check with your teachers what they expect of you to keep those particular options open.

Few people are good at everything, and if you don't take certain subjects or your grades are poor, there will be career implications. In part three of this book, you will find information about getting started in many different careers – including, where appropriate, advice on any specific subjects required. If in doubt, check further with the professional bodies listed, use the resources listed in chapter ten, or look in your Connexions/careers library. See what you can find out about the actual entry requirements for courses or careers which interest you. Never make a guess about the suitability of particular subjects for future careers! Always check.

All is not lost...

If you feel that you have made the wrong choice of subjects, or end up not doing as well as you hoped, it's not a disaster!

- In sixth forms and further education colleges you can take or retake GCSEs or other qualifications either on their own or alongside other courses.

- Although subjects such as languages, maths and the sciences need a good foundation before you can take them further, subjects like business studies and psychology can often be started from scratch at the advanced-level stage, or even at university!

- For entry to many courses and careers, GCSE-equivalent qualifications – such as BTEC Firsts, OCR level 2 Nationals, NVQs at level 2 – are often acceptable. These are available in further education colleges, some sixth forms, and, even through work-based learning in certain cases.

- In some circumstances, appropriate functional skill awards or key skills may be accepted in place of GCSE English, maths or ICT. Similarly, free-standing maths qualifications may be accepted instead of GCSE maths.

- Because they involve a lot of written work, humanities subjects are sometimes acceptable as evidence of your ability in English, even if you don't get a good grade in English itself.

- For some jobs, you can sit special tests or exams set by employers or professional bodies as alternatives to GCSEs.

- If you go into employment at the age of 16 or 17 without qualifications, you have the right to reasonable paid time off for study or training to gain a level 2 qualification. Your Connexions/careers service will have details.

- When you are older, course providers, universities and employers will often take your work experience into consideration, so the qualifications you achieved in school will be less important.

Chapter six

GCSEs subject by subject

Chapter five explains which subjects are compulsory and which are optional under the National Curriculum. Now you need to think about specific GCSE subjects in more detail. This chapter looks at the GCSE subjects likely to be offered in your school. First, we'll tell you a little more about GCSEs themselves.

What are GCSEs?

GCSE stands for General Certificate of Secondary Education. GCSEs were developed around 20 years ago. Although you don't have to take GCSEs, most students will sit at least a few. In 2007, almost six million GCSEs were taken by around half a million students!

- The normal age for sitting GCSEs is 16+, at the end of year 11. You can, however, take them earlier, later, or more than once, if you are advised to by your teachers.

- GCSEs are offered through the main examining boards – AQA, OCR, Edexcel, CCEA and WJEC. Schools are free to choose exam boards, so you could sit GCSEs from more than one.

- Where there is more than one GCSE in a subject (e.g. in different periods of history), your school will normally decide which you take.

- As described in chapter five, you can take GCSEs alongside other qualifications.

Remember, in many ways, what you actually learn on your GCSE course is far more valuable than any piece of paper. However, certificates do tell other people (employers, colleges etc) what subjects you have studied and the level you have reached in them.

Changes to GCSEs

As part of wider educational reforms, regulators in England, Wales and Northern Ireland have recently reviewed and changed many GCSEs in order to make them more relevant and interesting, develop your skills and ensure that work submitted for assessment is your own. In some cases, applied and general pathways are being made available within the same GCSE qualification. *Over the next few years, there may be further changes, so check that the information you read is as up to date as possible.*

Most of the 'new' GCSEs will be taught from 2009. However, new GCSEs in English, English literature, ICT and maths will be taught from 2010. Science GCSEs are already based on new programmes of study. Where possible, information on the 'new' GCSE courses is provided in this chapter.

GCSE assessment methods

GCSE exams

All GCSEs have at least some marks based on written exams – a few subjects are only assessed by exams.

When it comes to written exams, they probably won't be a new experience for you. For instance, throughout most of your schooling, you may have had your progress in some subjects assessed through national tests. Taking your GCSE exams will just be an extension of this.

GCSE exam papers usually have a broad range of question styles so that you can demonstrate what you know, understand and can do.

GCSE controlled assessments

Controlled assessment is replacing coursework in many GCSE subjects. This will ensure that the work submitted is your own.

- For most subjects, tasks will be set by exam boards, but may be adapted by schools depending on local issues and the resources available. Tasks will normally change each year.

- Most of your work on the tasks will be supervised, but there may be more limited supervision for research and group work. Your teacher will authenticate your work.

- In some subjects, exam boards will mark your work. However, this will usually be done by your teacher and then checked by the exam board.

Some GCSE subjects have just one controlled assessment unit or component making up 25% of the overall marks. For other, more practical or creative subjects, 60% of the marks will be based on controlled assessments.

GCSE coursework

Despite the introduction of controlled assessments, some GCSEs still have coursework components. Coursework is important because it assesses what you can do outside a written exam. You may have to juggle your time as you may have more than one piece of coursework on the go. If you feel snowed under, talk it over with your subject teachers who will help you organise your time.

GCSE grades

For full GCSEs and GCSE (short courses), there are eight grades from A* to G that are passes and a 'U' (ungraded) category. If you take a double-award GCSE (e.g. in an applied subject), you are graded from A*A* to GG.

- Grades D-G are at level 1.
- Grades A*-C are at level 2 and are needed for entry to many careers and courses.

GCSE tiering

Some GCSEs are tiered to give you the opportunity to show what you know, understand and can do at a particular band of attainment. In higher tier exam papers, controlled assessments etc, the questions may be more open-ended than in the foundation tier, for example.

If a subject has two tiers, the exams will cover either:

- the higher tier – grades A*-D, or
- the foundation tier – grades C-G. Examples of subjects with two tiers include maths, ICT, science, English and geography.

You and your subject teacher will decide which GCSE tier is most suitable for you.

Modular courses

Increasingly, GCSEs are available as modular courses. This means that they are broken up into units and each unit is assessed at different times throughout the course. If you feel that you could have done better in any of the units, you can resit these and your best results will count towards your final grade.

If you have taken a modular GCSE, your results slip will have 'UMS' (uniform mark scale) on it. UMS is the system exam boards use to combine marks to give your overall GCSE grade.

Key skills and functional skills

Key/functional skills can be developed through all GCSE subjects. For more information, see chapter five.

From September 2010, English, maths and ICT GCSEs will include the relevant functional skill. In order to ensure that students have the skills employers see as essential, the intention is that you will eventually need to pass functional skills at level 2 in order to pass the appropriate GCSE at grade A*-C.

Making GCSEs fair

How does anyone know that a GCSE grade C in English achieved in Berwick-on-Tweed is equivalent to a grade C in English taken in Bristol? To ensure fairness and equality, GCSEs have certain safeguards which apply to the qualification as a whole and to individual subjects.

- No matter which exam board is used, each GCSE has a set of national standards which are laid down by the Qualifications and Curriculum Authority. Each set of standards sets out what you will be assessed upon, and how that assessment will take place.

- Although coursework may be marked by your teachers, there are external checks to ensure that their assessment of your work is fair. Controlled assessments, as mentioned above, are being introduced in many subjects to ensure that the work is your own.

- There are various procedures in place to ensure that your written exams are marked consistently and that your final grade is fair. Examiners are trained and their marking checked; the exam board makes further checks.

- Once all the marking has taken place, there's a meeting to decide the number of marks needed to get each grade. There's even more regulation after this.

- If you or your teachers are not happy with the grade you've been awarded and feel something isn't right, your school can make a request for your paper to be re-marked or for the marks to be added up again. After this, if you are still unhappy about the mark, you can appeal.

Assessment arrangements may be adjusted, e.g. for students who speak English as a second language and for those with disabilities (including learning disabilities, such as dyslexia). You should discuss your requirements with your teachers well in advance.

Nearer the exams, if something happens outside your control that may affect your performance, such as a family crisis or illness, you could apply for special consideration. Speak to your teacher/s as soon as possible before or after the exam.

What next?

Find out from your school which GCSEs are available and from which exam boards. Check whether there are any restrictions on taking subjects that are considered too similar in content and whether timetabling clashes could affect which subjects you can do. Ask your teacher if he or she can show you the full course details.

The main GCSE subject areas

GCSEs are available in over 45 subjects. The rest of this chapter looks at the main GCSE subject areas to give you a flavour of the programmes of study. However, you should not assume that every aspect of each subject is described.

The subject areas described in this chapter are:

- art and design
- business
- citizenship
- design and technology
- engineering
- English
- geography
- health and social care

- history
- home economics
- information and communication technology
- leisure and tourism
- mathematics
- media
- modern foreign languages
- music
- performing arts
- physical education
- religious studies
- science
- social sciences
- Welsh.

For each subject area, you will find information on:

- the GCSE courses available
- why you should consider studying the subject
- the type of things you will learn
- how the subject is assessed
- what kind of careers the subject is required for, or useful for.

Apart from the GCSEs mentioned in this chapter, your school may offer many others, including:

- archaeology
- Biblical Hebrew
- classical Greek
- construction and the built environment
- general studies
- hospitality and catering
- humanities

- Latin
- manufacturing
- modern Hebrew.

Art and design

You may be able to take **art and design GCSE**, a **GCSE (short course)**, or **GCSE applied art and design**. Applied art and design is a work-related qualification. It is available as a single award (equivalent to one GCSE) or a double award (equivalent to two GCSEs).

In art and design GCSE, you can follow a broad course in

art and design or choose from fine art, graphic communication, textile design, three-dimensional design, critical and contextual studies or photography: lens- and light-based media.

Why study art and design?

GCSE art and design will develop your creativity and imagination, and encourage you to express and communicate your ideas effectively through the various media. You will learn about present-day art and design, and that of other cultures and other times.

The applied course will allow you to develop your interest in art and design in a more work-related context. You'll get the chance to study the work practices of individual artists and designers.

What will I learn?

In art and design GCSE you will learn:

- how to be creative from an idea, from what you observe or from a past experience
- about a range of art, craft and design processes
- how to use different materials and techniques, colours and forms

- how ideas, feelings and meanings can be expressed through different media.

In applied art and design you will:

- learn how artists and designers work

- experiment with different media and materials to put your ideas across

- acquire practical skills and techniques through working on a design brief

- study the work practices of individuals and small businesses.

Assessment

For GCSE art and design, 60% of your marks are based on controlled assessment (such as developing a portfolio of artwork) and 40% is based on external assessment.

Career link

Besides the obvious occupations, such as, fashion, graphic, exhibition, jewellery and interior design, art and design may also be useful for computer-aided design, media careers, architecture, floristry, landscape design, special effects work, work in hairdressing and beauty and many other careers.

Business

You may be able to take **GCSE business studies, GCSE business studies (short course), GCSE applied business, GCSE economics** or **GCSE economics (short course)**. Your school may offer related GCSEs, such as **business studies and economics** or **business and communication systems**.

GCSE applied business is a work-related qualification. It is available as a single or double award (worth either one or two GCSEs respectively).

Why study business?

Business is a subject that is relevant to our everyday lives. If you enjoy keeping up with what's happening in the outside world, or fancy yourself as the next Alan Sugar, it could be a subject that will appeal to you!

What will I learn?

In GCSE business studies, you will:

- learn about business activities and the reasons why some businesses succeed, while others fail
- investigate the effects businesses have on society, including business ethics and sustainability
- learn about customers – this may include learning about marketing and market research
- investigate how businesses use information to make decisions and solve problems
- learn about ICT and how it is used in business.

GCSE applied business covers similar topics; you also develop your knowledge by studying a range of businesses – these may be based in your local area or all over the country. Applied business has a practical approach and involves developing relevant skills, such as organising your time and presenting information in different ways.

GCSE economics involves learning about different theories of economic behaviour as well as the effects of business competition, and how economic information is used.

Assessment

In GCSE business studies, 75% of your mark is assessed through written exams. The other 25% is through controlled assessment.

In GCSE applied business, 60% of the course is assessed through controlled assessment and 40% through external assessment.

GCSE economics is assessed entirely through exams.

Career link

Studying business is useful if you are interested in any career in business, whether in finance, marketing or retailing, to name just a few. There is a wide range of business-related courses after year 11 and at university. However, it's not usually necessary to have previously studied business.

You should be aware of the difference between business studies and courses in administration and office skills. These courses may lead to careers in support roles, such as receptionist, secretary or clerical assistant. Although there are GCSEs which include aspects of office skills, you are more likely to take specialist qualifications, such as those offered by OCR or City & Guilds.

Citizenship

A GCSE in citizenship studies is offered as a **GCSE (short course)**. A short course counts as half a full GCSE. From September 2009, a **full GCSE in citizenship studies** will also be available.

Why study citizenship?

None of us lives in isolation. We are part of a national and international community, living and working together. Citizenship studies will look at what is happening around you, and help you to form opinions. You will look at the wider picture of how communities and governments work, and your rights and responsibilities. It is also a good starting off point for studying social sciences after year 11.

What will I learn?

During citizenship studies, you will learn:

- to explore local, national and international issues of current interest

- how democracy works

- about justice, as well as your rights and responsibilities

- to interpret different kinds of information from the media and recognise facts, opinions and bias

- to form and express your own opinions both in speech and in writing
- how to become involved in, and contribute to, citizenship activities.

Assessment

Exams makes up 40% of the total marks and controlled assessment makes up 60%.

Career link

Citizenship studies will be useful in a wide variety of careers including media, journalism, social work, politics, local government and law.

Design and technology

GCSE design and technology courses which may be available in your school include:

- electronic products
- food technology
- graphic products or graphics

- product design

- resistant materials technology or resistant materials

- systems and control technology or control systems

- textiles technology.

Instead of taking a full GCSE course, you may be able to take a **GCSE design and technology (short course)** in one or more of the areas listed above.

In addition, there are courses in subjects related to design and technology, such as **GCSE electronics**.

If you are interested in taking more than one design and technology course, check the details of each course with your teachers as there are likely to be some restrictions on taking subjects that are too similar.

Why study design and technology?

Design and technology will be of particular interest to you if you are practical and creative. In today's rapidly changing society, it is important that you acquire knowledge and skills that relate to today's technological world.

What will I learn?

In a design and technology course, you:

- create proposals and plans for products to meet design briefs

- consider the work of other designers when creating your own products

- learn to safely use a range of tools and equipment (including new technology, such as CAD and CAM) to design and make different products

- consider how design and technology is affected by ethical, environmental, and social issues

- analyse finished products and try to come up with answers to problems and needs.

Assessment

Exams make up 40% of your total marks and controlled assessment makes up 60%.

Career link

If you are interested in a career in a particular area of design and technology, such as electronics or food technology, it makes sense to choose the course that focuses on that subject. However, it is not essential to take GCSE design and technology in order to enter a career in the area. Any of the design and technology courses will give you a broad base from which you could later go on to specialist training.

Engineering

GCSE engineering is a work-related qualification. It is available as a single award (equivalent to one GCSE) and a double award (equivalent to two GCSEs).

Why study engineering?

This is a subject that gives you the chance to undertake practical projects and to find solutions to engineering problems. Even if you do not eventually choose a career in engineering, the course will give you an insight into a large sector of UK industry and improve your problem solving and other skills.

What will I learn?

Both single and double award courses include learning about:

- product analysis
- how to engineer a product
- different engineering processes.

If you choose to study the double award then you will:

- investigate the real world of engineering
- make an engineered product
- learn about engineering for sustainability.

You will develop skills, knowledge and understanding which you would be able to use in the engineering industry. You will learn about the materials used (like plastics, metals and ceramics), different engineering processes, how engineers control quality and how new technologies have affected the design and manufacture of products. The course also allows you to learn how to use tools and equipment safely.

Assessment

40% of your marks are made up of external assessment and 60% by controlled assessment.

Career link

GCSE engineering is a good basis for progression to an Apprenticeship in engineering, or on to advanced, further and higher education courses in the subject – although maths and science may be the main requirements for entry to many courses. Different branches of engineering include mechanical, electronic, chemical, marine and medical engineering.

English

You can take **GCSE English** and **GCSE English literature**. There are two tiers in English and English literature and your teacher will advise you which one you should be entered for. N.B. From 2010, there are plans to offer you the choice between either new GCSEs in English language and English literature, or a more functional English GCSE.

Why study English?

Whatever you want to do in the future, you will need English. English literature will appeal to you if you enjoy reading books for pleasure.

What will I learn?

In English, you will learn to:

- speak and listen effectively – you will learn how to express yourself and your ideas clearly in different situations, using appropriate vocabulary, as well as responding to other people and showing you understand them

- read a range of different material including prose, poetry and drama – understanding and responding to text from different cultures

- write effectively including how to communicate different meanings, how to structure writing using grammar and punctuation and how to write for different readers and purposes.

In English literature you will:

- read, understand and respond to lots of different literary texts, including drama, prose and poetry

- explore the ways authors achieve different effects

- learn how to show meaning in writing and speech and how this can be adapted for different audiences

- learn how to relate texts to their social, historical and cultural contexts.

Assessment

In GCSE English, exams account for between 50-60% of your overall mark, with the remaining marks gained through controlled assessment.

In GCSE English literature, exams account for between 50-70% of your overall mark, with the remaining marks gained through controlled assessment.

Career link

English is necessary for every job and the ability to communicate, both orally and in writing, is of great importance in everyday life.

You will find that English GCSE at grade A*-C is specified for training in many careers and is required by many employers.

Geography

As well as **geography GCSE**, your school may offer you the opportunity to take a **GCSE (short course)** in this subject.

There are two different GCSE courses – the topics you will study depend on the particular GCSE course offered by your school. You therefore need to look carefully at your school's course information.

Why study geography?

The aim of geography GCSE is to give you an understanding of the world you live in, not only the physical environment – but also landscapes, the climate and also how human beings interact with the environment. It is a subject that is very relevant to our lives today, and to the decisions that are being made daily about the way the world should be developed and protected.

What will I learn?

In geography GCSE, you will learn:

- about the relationship between human beings and the environment

- how to carry out fieldwork and collect different types of information
- about current issues, like climate change and sustainable development
- about physical and human geography.

Assessment

75% of your marks are made up of external assessment and 25% by controlled assessment, which may include fieldwork.

Career link

Geography is relevant to many careers. Architecture, landscape architecture, travel and tourism, logistics and transport, forestry, cartography, agriculture, planning, housing management, geology, meteorology, surveying and environmental work are all examples of career areas where geographical skills and knowledge are useful.

Health and social care

GCSE health and social care is a work-related qualification. It is available as either a single or double award (equivalent to two GCSEs).

Why study health and social care?

This course allows you to find out how, as individuals, we all grow and develop and how this affects our needs for health and social care. It is a useful subject to take if you are interested in finding out about the different types of work involved in caring for people, and how health and social services are organised.

What will I learn?

In health and social care, you will:

- investigate the services available for healthcare, social care and early years care
- consider the barriers that can prevent people from gaining the care they need
- learn about the many different jobs in health and social care, and the skills they require

- study the different stages in a person's life and the things that affect their growth and development
- examine the various types of relationships we form with other people.

In addition, on the double award course, you will:

- find out which factors can have a positive or negative effect on our health and wellbeing
- investigate how to measure a person's health
- learn about how to motivate and support a person in improving their health.

Assessment

Exams count for 40% of your overall mark, while controlled assessments count for 60%. A controlled assessment may, for example, involve you producing a report showing the type of care an individual might need, based on researching their needs and the services available.

Career link

Health and social care is useful if you are interested in working with people (such as children, adults, older people, or any group of individuals with particular needs, such as disabled people) in a caring way.

History

As well as **history GCSE**, your school may offer you the opportunity to take a **GCSE (short course)** qualification in this subject. **GCSE classical civilisation** or **ancient history** may also be available at some schools.

Why study history?

History can be fascinating as you discover how different life used to be. You will find out how things such as medicine, warfare, laws, technology, human rights, fashion, attitudes and so on, have changed over time and within different societies. Studying history also helps us understand the 'here and now'; how events of the past have shaped the world of today.

What will I learn?

In history GCSE, you will:

- study particular topics, themes or periods in history
- learn about the key people, events and developments involved at the time
- discover the links between the past and present
- explore the subject using books, paintings, photographs, music, spoken stories, historical objects and buildings
- learn how to analyse and interpret information and draw conclusions from it
- question why different people have different views on the same events
- learn how to present and communicate your findings clearly.

There are two different GCSE courses: modern world history and schools history project. The kind of history or the periods you will study depend on the particular history GCSE course offered by your school. You therefore need to look carefully at your school's course information.

Assessment

75% of your overall mark is assessed through exams and 25% through controlled assessment.

Career link

History is particularly relevant if you are interested in museum work, archaeology, conservation/restoration or archive work. The skills that you develop in evaluating and organising information, as well as having a knowledge of history, are also useful for careers such as law, architecture, library work, planning, the media and for creative work of all kinds.

Teaching history in schools is a major area of employment for historians. Lecturing in universities is also a possibility, where teaching is usually carried out alongside research. For this, you would need to take your history studies beyond degree level.

Home economics

You can study this subject as **GCSE home economics**, or you can specialise in one of the following:

- **GCSE home economics: textiles**
- **GCSE home economics: food and nutrition**
- **GCSE home economics: child development**.

Why study home economics?

This will appeal to you if you are interested in human needs, understanding about healthy living and the influence that society, economics and our environment has on us as consumers. You may also learn either about family life, diet and health or other specialised subjects depending on the particular options that your school offers. Theory and practice are important as you learn to use equipment, solve problems and make decisions.

What will I learn?

In home economics, you will learn:

- how to manage your resources effectively and make informed choices
- about human needs at various stages of life

- which factors can affect the quality of our lives
- how technological and scientific changes influence the home
- good safety practices.

Assessment

Controlled assessments make up 60% of your overall mark and include research, planning and practical activities (such as a study of a child's development or preparing a meal); 40% will be assessed through a written exam.

Career link

Home economics as a GCSE subject is not essential to any career, but it is very useful if you are interested in childcare, catering, dietetics and nutrition, and service industries. And we all, at some stage in our lives, must look after ourselves, make a home and perhaps raise a family.

Information and communication technology (ICT)

You may be able to take **GCSE ICT**, the **GCSE (short course)** and, in some schools, **GCSE applied ICT**. The applied course is a work-related qualification that leads to a double award (equivalent to two GCSEs).

Why study ICT?

ICT plays a major part in just about every aspect of our lives – at school or college, at work, at home, and out and about. New and better ways of using computers, the internet, mobile phones and other telecommunications are constantly being developed. While you will learn ICT skills through other subjects on the curriculum, if you want more than the basic knowledge, then taking ICT as a GCSE subject might be a good idea.

The applied ICT course is more heavily work-related, and takes double the time. It will therefore suit you if you want to commit a lot of your studies to ICT, and intend to go into related employment or to follow vocational further and higher education courses.

What will I learn?

The GCSE ICT course covers:

- applying your knowledge, skills and understanding of ICT in various situations

- understanding the ways ICT is used, and the impact of its uses

- analysing, designing, implementing, testing and evaluating ICT systems

- understanding social, legal, ethical and other issues raised by the use of ICT.

The applied ICT course covers the same ground, with more emphasis on the working environment, and is made up of three units: ICT tools and applications, ICT in organisations, and ICT and society.

Assessment

For GCSE ICT, between 40% and 60% of your mark is based on coursework, with the rest based on a final exam. In the applied course, coursework can count for up to 85% of your mark, with external assessment carrying between 15% and 34%.

Career link

It is not necessary to have a GCSE pass in ICT to work in computing, but it will provide a useful basis if you decide to continue studying the subject to AS/A level, or equivalent. For computer engineering or even computer science, the more important subjects are maths and physics (or science and additional science). But ICT is likely to be appreciated by all sorts of employers whose businesses use computer systems.

Leisure and tourism

GCSE leisure and tourism is a work-related qualification. It is available as either a single or double award (equivalent to two GCSEs).

Why study leisure and tourism?

You may already know something about leisure and tourism – as a customer who has taken a holiday or visited a theme park, for example. Studying it as a GCSE subject will appeal to you if you are interested in finding out more about the industry, in planning and carrying out your own investigations, and in learning about business.

What will I learn?

In leisure and tourism you will:

- examine how the industry is changing

- identify how different attitudes and cultures affect leisure and tourism

- learn about sustainable leisure and tourism, environmental issues, and health and safety

- investigate what customers want and why they make the choices they do

- discover the different types of jobs and organisations within the industry, and how they operate.

Assessment

There are two units within the single award course, and four units within the double. Overall, controlled assessments count for 60% of your mark, and written exams for 40%.

Career link

Studying leisure and tourism will be useful for a wide range of careers within the leisure and tourism industry, as well as for many other businesses.

Mathematics

GCSE maths has two tiers – foundation and higher. Your teacher will talk to you about the appropriate tier for you. Your school may also offer **GCSE statistics**.

Why study mathematics?

Maths is one of your most important subjects. A huge range of jobs, as well as most further and higher education courses, require you to have achieved a grade A*-C in GCSE mathematics.

Studying maths helps you to understand other subjects, like science, engineering or design and technology. And throughout your life, being numerate, that is, having confidence in dealing with numbers, will be essential in all sorts of situations. From calculating how many cans of paint you need to buy to decorate your bedroom, to understanding your mortgage interest payments – maths is crucial!

What will I learn?

By the end of the course, you should be able to:

- solve problems using maths, if necessary by using calculators or computers

- understand numbers (such as decimals, fractions and percentages)

- understand algebra

- deal with shapes, spaces and measuring (such as angles, circles and areas)

- handle data (for example, looking for trends)

- understand how maths is relevant to our daily lives.

Assessment

Your mark is based entirely on exams. You are required to sit two separate exams – one of which allows the use of a calculator.

Career link

Maths at grade A*-C is essential for entry to teacher training, and for most jobs and higher education courses in science, medicine, healthcare, architecture or engineering. It is also likely to be asked for if you want to work in financial services, such as insurance or banking, in administration, or in ICT.

Media

GCSE media studies is available as either a single or double award (equivalent to two GCSEs). In some schools the teaching of media studies may be overlapped with the teaching of English.

Why study media?

If you are interested in how such things as newspapers, films, radio shows, podcasts and comics are produced, and in how people relate to them, then GCSE media studies will appeal to you. The approach to learning is very practical and involves analysing different types of media and producing your own portfolio of work.

What will I learn?

You will:

- study at least three different forms of media (including at least one print based and one audio-visual based)
- learn about the range of industries and types of jobs involved in the media
- investigate the role of mass media in society
- look for evidence of bias in different media
- consider how the media represents different groups of people
- develop practical skills and work creatively
- learn how different communication styles are used for different audiences
- examine the changes in media technology.

Assessment

A range of controlled assessments counts for 60% of your mark, while 40% is based on exams. The controlled assessments may involve some group work to produce a portfolio of print-based or electronic media products and supporting materials.

Career link

GCSE media studies is useful, but not essential, for a wide range of roles in the media industries, such as newspapers, advertising, the web, TV and radio.

Modern foreign languages

The most widely taught GCSE languages are **French**, **Spanish** and **German** – but your school may offer something different, such as **Russian**, **Japanese**, **Urdu** or **Chinese**. You may have the choice of following a **GCSE (short course)** that focuses on either just the spoken language or just the written language.

Why study a modern foreign language?

There are lots of good reasons! You only have to spend a holiday abroad to find out how useful it is to speak another language. Being able to communicate in one or more foreign languages also increases your opportunities for working or studying abroad when you are older.

But it's not just a matter of speaking or writing a different language. Studying a modern foreign language will also introduce you to the culture of that country.

If you are keen to study languages at university, you should aim to take more than one language at GCSE – two full GCSEs, or perhaps one full course and one GCSE (short course).

What will I learn?

By the end of the course, you should be able to:

- hold a conversation with someone in the foreign language
- read and write the language
- use a wide range of vocabulary suitable for a variety of different situations

- use the correct grammar
- understand the culture of the countries or communities where the language is spoken.

Assessment

Exams count for 40% of your overall mark and test your ability to understand a language when reading or listening to it. Controlled assessments count for 60% or your mark, and include several speaking and writing tasks.

Career link

Languages are particularly useful for work in travel and tourism, hospitality, some departments of the Civil Service, teaching, journalism, librarianship and the arts as well as in industry and commerce. Translating and interpreting are about the only jobs which rely on language skills and not much else. Usually, you will need other skills – such as technical, administrative or secretarial skills – to use alongside your languages. Languages are particularly helpful in getting jobs overseas or with multinational companies.

You can study the more unusual languages, like Arabic or Vietnamese, at university from scratch. But you will usually need to have at least one GCSE and A level in a modern foreign language to show that you are good at learning languages.

Music

If you have enjoyed learning to sing or play a musical instrument either at school or in your spare time, **GCSE music** will give you the chance to develop your knowledge of music theory as well as your practical skills.

Why study music?

Music at GCSE level can be a basis for further study of the subject, or may just give you a knowledge and understanding of music that will help you appreciate it for the rest of your life.

What will I learn?

In GCSE music you will:

- learn about the language of music – rhythm, melody, harmony and so on

- listen to and appraise a range of music styles, such as classical, African, jazz, film music, hip hop, Bhangra, or pop songs

- learn about the technology used in music

- compose music, either in your own style or to meet a brief that you have been given

- perform music – there is great flexibility in the type of performances you may work on – solo, group, DJing, rapping, live or sequencing, for example!

Assessment

Assessment is through a combination of exams and controlled assessments. Between 60% and 70% of your mark is based on performance and composing. The remainder of the mark is based on your ability to listen to and appraise different music.

Career link

If you are having music lessons out of school, and want to concentrate on performance, getting high grades in practical music exams can be more important than GCSE. However, a GCSE at grade A*-C in music can provide the basis for studying music at AS and A level, which you will need if you intend to go on to study music at university. Apart from performing, there are many other careers where your knowledge of music will be useful – such as arts administration, music librarianship, sound recording, broadcasting, journalism and music publishing.

Performing arts

There are **GCSEs in drama** and **dance**. Your school may also offer **GCSE expressive arts** which may include many different art forms like dance, drama, music, visual arts, writing (including poetry) and moving images (including films).

Why study performing arts?

You will want to study these courses if you like a subject which involves a lot of teamwork and is both practical and creative. It gives you the opportunity – both in the limelight and behind the scenes – to learn about the many different aspects of putting a performance together. Performing arts can also introduce you to different forms of art from various cultures. It can also give you plenty of personal satisfaction and spark off a lifelong leisure interest.

What will I learn?

In drama GCSE, you will learn:

- to use drama to express your feelings and ideas, taking part in both scripted work and improvisation

- how to interpret a character or role

- what practical and technical skills are required to put on a performance in front of an audience.

In dance GCSE you will learn:

- about a range of dance styles and how to perform them

- about choreography

- how to express your ideas and instructions

- how to rate dance performances.

Assessment

For GCSEs in dance, drama and expressive arts, 60% of your marks are based on controlled assessment – this may involve a practical performance and some written evidence. External assessment counts for 40% of your marks.

Career link

Dance, drama and expressive arts as GCSE subjects are not there to produce actors, dancers or stage technicians. However, if you are interested in a career in these areas, a GCSE can be a useful introduction.

These subjects can also teach you skills such as, self-confidence, teamwork, problem solving and communication, which employers look for in a wide range of careers. These include jobs where meeting people face to face is particularly important, for example, retail, travel and tourism, sales and marketing.

Physical education (PE)

GCSE PE combines theoretical knowledge with active participation in selected sports or games. Your school may also offer PE as a **GCSE (short course)** or **double award** (worth two GCSEs).

Why study PE?

A GCSE in PE will give you a good understanding about the importance of a healthy and active lifestyle. PE can help your self confidence, improve your teamwork and leadership skills, and keep you fit!

What will I learn?

During GCSE PE you will:

- develop your skills in at least two sporting or physical activities, such as gymnastics, team games, dance, athletics, adventure activities, swimming or fitness training

- take on the different roles of player/performer, coach, team leader and official

- learn about the health benefits and safety risks of physical activities

- learn to analyse both your own and other people's performance

- study anatomy and physiology

- plan exercise and training programmes.

Assessment

Controlled assessments count for 60% of your overall mark and include performing in your chosen sporting or physical activities. Written exams count for the remaining 40% of your mark.

Career link

GCSE PE, alongside other subjects such as maths, English and science, can be useful for entry to further and higher education courses in sport and fitness, or if you wish to go straight into employment in the sport and leisure industry.

Religious studies

As well as **GCSE religious studies**, your school may also offer a **GCSE (short course)**.

Why study religious studies?

GCSE religious studies is open to people of all religions and those with no religious faith at all. The GCSE course is based on developing your knowledge and understanding of one or more of the main religions, and taking time to reflect on your own beliefs. If you are interested in finding out more about religious faiths and spirituality, and you enjoy discussing ethical and moral issues, religious studies GCSE will appeal to you.

What will I learn?

In religious studies GCSE, you will:

- learn about the key beliefs, traditions and forms of worship of at least one, and often of more than one, religion (depending on the particular GCSE course offered at your school)

- consider how religions influence what people experience, believe and do

- consider important questions about life – including issues such as world poverty, euthanasia or life after death – and explore the answers that religion provides.

Assessment

Your mark is based entirely on written exams.

Career link

Religious studies provides a good background for any career where understanding people is an asset, including social work, teaching, youth work, journalism, probation work, the police, broadcasting, the medical and caring professions and human resource management. It is obviously relevant if you are thinking of going into any kind of religious work.

Science

There are several science-related GCSEs that you may be able to take either separately or in combination with one another. **GCSE science** is the most widely available course and gives you an introduction to biology, physics and chemistry. It can be studied on its own, but often it will be taken with a second science subject. Depending on what your school offers, your second science subject may be:

- **GCSE additional science** – this builds on your skills and knowledge across all three areas of biology, physics and chemistry

- **GCSE additional applied science** – this takes a more work-related approach to the sciences

- **GCSE biology, GCSE physics** or **GCSE chemistry** – these allow you to study each subject in more depth.

GCSE applied science (double award) is worth two GCSEs and includes science theory but concentrates mostly on how science applies to the workplace and on developing practical skills.

A few schools may offer you the option of taking GCSEs in all three science subjects together, that is: GCSE biology, GCSE physics and GCSE chemistry.

Other science-related GCSE subjects that may be available to you include: **human health and physiology**, **electronics**, **environmental science**, **astronomy**, **geology**, and **environmental and land-based science**.

How much science to take?

While GCSE science is useful as part of your general education, on its own it will not provide an adequate basis for further study in science. If there is any possibility that you might want to continue with science beyond 16, a second science subject is a must, otherwise your career openings will be severely limited. Use the careers guide later in this book to *check exactly which science subjects will be required for different jobs.*

If you choose to take three science GCSEs, by focusing so heavily on the sciences you may be missing out on other subjects that could be useful to you further down the line.

Why study science?

The work of scientists, past and present, touches nearly every aspect of our lives: medicine, farming, technology, food, textiles, the environment, energy, sport and so on! Gaining an understanding of science is therefore extremely important to us all. It is also hugely important for our economy to have knowledgeable and highly-skilled scientists working in research and industry.

What will I learn?

In GCSE science, you will:

- learn about living things – humans, plants and animals
- study chemicals and materials, and how they behave
- investigate different types of energy and how we can generate energy from different processes
- learn about the environment and the impact that humans have on it
- learn about Earth and the universe
- carry out practical activities and investigations
- analyse and interpret experimental results
- consider the impact of science on our society.

In GCSE applied science (double award), you will:

- learn how science is used in the workplace
- examine how science can be applied to meet the changing needs of society
- develop the practical skill needed for scientific investigations and analysis
- learn how to work safely in science.

Assessment

In GCSE science, assessment is through exams and also through coursework, which may account for 20-30% of your total marks.

In GCSE applied science (double award), there are three equal units – two are assessed through coursework and one through an exam. The coursework may involve building up a portfolio. This could be which includes your assessed coursework.

Career link

If you are considering any career related to science, technology or engineering, it will be important to take GCSE science with an additional science, or GCSE applied science (double award). It is essential that you check the exact GCSE requirements for any careers that you are considering.

Examples of career areas where science is required or useful include:

- many careers in industry – including all aspects of engineering, the manufacturing industries, chemical and energy production, food production, pharmaceuticals, biotechnology, telecommunications and the land-based industries

- medically-related work – including, of course, being a doctor, vet or dentist, but also doing medical research, medical instrumentation and equipment design and development, pharmacy, dietetics, medical technology, bioscience and the allied health professions, such as physiotherapy or speech and language therapy

- environmental work – research, conservation and so on

- forensic science

- hairdressing

- catering

- science teaching in secondary school and beyond. Also, to train to teach in primary schools, you must have GCSE science at grade A*-C.

For scientific careers, you will need to take your science qualifications at least to A level or the equivalent, and, for many careers, to degree level.

Social sciences

You may have the option of studying one or more of the GCSE subjects that are often referred to as social sciences: **law, psychology** or **sociology**. Law GCSE is only available as a full course; however psychology and sociology can both be taken as a **GCSE (short course)**.

"No, it's not called socialising studies ..."

Why study social sciences?

Social sciences look at how societies operate, and how people live and relate to one another. These subjects will appeal to you if you are interested in people and how they behave. Psychology and sociology are also useful if you would like to learn about different ways of conducting research and analysing the results.

What will I learn?

- In GCSE law, you will learn about the role of the courts and the different legal professions, as well as how laws are made and enforced. You will also consider individual rights and responsibilities in different situations.

- In GCSE psychology, you will look into how things, such as biology, development, learning and reasoning affect how people think and behave. You will also investigate how psychological research relates to society as a whole.

- In GCSE sociology, you examine the trends in society, such as how families, employment and education have changed over time. You will look into why inequalities exist in society, who holds power and how this affects us all.

Assessment

In law, psychology and sociology, assessment is 100% by written exams.

Career link

These social sciences GCSEs can be very interesting subjects to take if you want to widen your outlook on society. However, although they may sound very work-related, it is important to understand that studying law, psychology and sociology at this level is not a requirement to work in these fields in the future.

Welsh

If you go to school in Wales, you will learn Welsh. If Welsh is your first language, you will take **GCSE Welsh first language**. If your first language is not Welsh, you will take **GCSE Welsh second language**. A **Welsh second language GCSE (short course)** may also be available. Your school may also offer **GCSE Welsh literature**.

Why study Welsh?

The Welsh language is widely spoken, especially in certain areas of Wales, and your ability to communicate in it will not only improve your job prospects, but will also make an important contribution to keeping the language, and the cultural heritage it represents, alive.

What will I learn?

In GCSE Welsh first or second language, you:

- develop interest, pleasure and enthusiasm for the Welsh language

- contribute to discussions using language appropriate for the purpose and audience

- respond (both orally and in writing) to a range of reading matter

- write in a wide range of ways for a variety of purposes, with attention to accuracy and audience.

In GCSE Welsh literature, you will:

- read and respond to literary material from different eras

- respond to a literary presentation produced for TV, radio, film, tape or disk

- develop the skills needed for studying literature, e.g. you will learn how authors use language to create effects

- respond to literature in a range of oral and written ways.

Assessment

In GCSE Welsh first language, a third of your marks are based on coursework, a third on an oral exam and a third on a written exam.

Coursework accounts for 40% of your total mark in GCSE Welsh second language. The final assessment counts for the remaining 60% of your marks and this is divided into three exams – an oral exam (20%), a listening comprehension exam (10%) and a written exam (30%).

In GCSE Welsh literature, 50% of your marks are based on a written exam, 20% on an oral exam and 30% on coursework.

Career link

More and more young people are fluent in Welsh and English and employers in Wales increasingly want people who can communicate in both languages. There's a particular demand for Welsh speakers in leisure and tourism, health and social services, the media etc.

If you are interested in studying languages at university, a knowledge of Welsh will show that you are capable of acquiring language skills.

Chapter seven

Diplomas

What are Diplomas?

Available at some schools and colleges in England, these new qualifications have been introduced to widen the range of options available to you. However, they don't replace existing qualifications, such as GCSEs. Although you learn about a broad area of work, Diplomas don't train you for a specific job, neither do they commit you to a job in the subject area studied.

Diplomas have been developed in partnership with employers, schools, colleges and universities. They combine classroom study with practical learning in different environments. Very few schools and colleges have the resources to offer all the Diploma subjects, so you may find yourself travelling to another school or college, or to an employer, to take all or part of your Diploma.

Diploma subjects

The Diploma subject areas already available are:

- construction and the built environment (covers a range of industries including architecture, surveying and the building trades)

- creative and media (introduces a wide range of subjects, including 2D/3D visual art, product design, fashion, advertising, dance, film and television, animation, creative writing, music and graphic design)

- engineering

- information technology

- society, health and development (includes the care of children and young people, health, community justice and social care).

From 2009, Diplomas will be available in:

- business, administration and finance
- environmental and land-based studies
- hair and beauty studies
- hospitality
- manufacturing and product design.

From 2010, Diplomas will be available in:

- public services
- retail
- sport and leisure
- travel and tourism.

From 2011, there are plans to introduce Diplomas in:

- humanities
- languages
- science.

Component parts

If you decide to take a Diploma at Key Stage 4, you will still study the compulsory National Curriculum subjects, such as English, maths, science and PE (see chapter five). Diplomas are made up of three main elements as described below.

Principal learning

You learn about your chosen broad employment sector. You'll take a certain number of compulsory units to develop your understanding and knowledge. This part of the Diploma should help you decide which areas you would like to specialise in.

Generic learning

This will give you the general skills that employers, colleges and universities require. It comprises:

- **functional skills** – you will learn to apply your English, maths and ICT skills to work and life situations

- **personal, learning and thinking skills**, e.g. teamwork, self-management, creative thinking and the ability to reflect on your learning

- a **project** related to your chosen employment sector – you will be able to explore in detail a topic that interests you

- **work experience** – you will receive at least ten days' structured work experience.

Additional or specialist learning

You will be able to select courses from a range of options. You can either:

- choose to study a topic in more detail, or

- broaden your learning, e.g. by taking a language or a subject like geography.

N.B. Qualifications, such as GCSEs and AS/A levels can be taken alongside a Diploma or included in the programme.

There may be some limits as to what you can study. It's possible that schools/colleges in your area are unable to offer a particular unit/course. You may not have the time to take all the extra units/courses you would like. Also, there may be restrictions because some subjects duplicate others too much.

Diploma levels

Diplomas can be taken at three levels. The first two levels can be taken at Key Stage 4; all levels are available post-16:

- **Foundation Diploma** – a level 1 qualification equivalent to five GCSEs at grades D-G

- **Higher Diploma** – a level 2 qualification equivalent to seven GCSEs at grades A*-C

- **Advanced Diploma** – a level 3 qualification equivalent to three and a half A levels. In addition, the **Progression Diploma** is equivalent to two and a half A levels.

Diplomas normally take two years of full-time study. If you take a Foundation or Higher Diploma post-16, you may be able to complete it in less time. It is possible to take a Diploma part time whilst working.

From 2011, **Extended Diplomas** are expected to be available at all the above levels in each subject area. As well as more opportunity for in-depth and independent research, there will also be a greater focus on English and maths. It's expected that the:

- Foundation Extended Diploma (level 1) will be equivalent to seven GCSEs

- Higher Extended Diploma (level 2) will be equivalent to nine GCSEs

- Advanced Extended Diploma (level 3) will be equivalent to four and a half A levels.

Assessment and grading

Diplomas are both externally and internally assessed. As appropriate, a range of internal assessment methods are used.

To achieve the overall Diploma qualification, you have to pass all the component parts as listed earlier. An overall grade is based on how well you do in the principal learning and the project. Grades will be given as follows:

- Foundation Diploma – A*, A, B or U (ungraded)
- Higher Diploma – A*, A, B, C or U
- Advanced Diploma – A*-E or U.

When you have finished your course, you will get a 'Diploma transcript'. This will provide a record of all you achievements in the various parts of the Diploma programme.

Progression

Once you have completed your Diploma, you can progress in a number of ways. For instance, you could:

- move up to the next Diploma level (in the same subject or a different one)

- take another related or unrelated course at school, college or university (Advanced Diplomas attract UCAS Tariff points for university entrance)

- start a job with training, e.g. an Apprenticeship.

Find out more

For more information about Diplomas, talk to your teachers and/or Connexions personal adviser. Lots of information can be found on: http://yp.direct.gov.uk/diplomas

Chapter eight

Looking into the future

The courses you are taking for the next two years should be enjoyable, but they're not just there for fun! They measure your performance and prepare the way for the next stage.

Think of qualifications as keys which will open certain doors. The difficulty is that you may not be sure yet which doors you want to open. Therefore you don't know which keys to choose. Obviously the bigger the bunch, the more doors you will be able to open!

After year 11 the main options open to you will be:

- continuing with full-time learning at school or college
- getting a job and learning in the workplace.

N.B. In the future, the Government wants all young people to stay in some form of education or training until they reach the age of 18.

The National Qualifications Framework (NQF)

To ensure that learners and employers can easily compare qualifications at different levels, most have been fitted into the NQF. Qualifications at the same level have similar standards.

Qualification level	Examples of qualifications at this NQF level
7/8	Doctorate, masters degree, postgraduate certificate/diploma, NVQ level 5
6	Honours degree, graduate certificate/diploma, NVQ level 4
5	HNC/HND, foundation degree, Diploma of Higher Education, NVQ level 4
4	Certificate of Higher Education, NVQ level 4
3	AS/A level, Advanced/Progression Diploma, BTEC National, OCR level 3 National, International Baccalaureate Diploma, Welsh Baccalaureate Advanced Diploma, Cambridge Pre-U, Extended Project, NVQ level 3
2	GCSE (grade A*-C), Higher Diploma, BTEC First, OCR level 2 National, Welsh Baccalaureate Intermediate Diploma, NVQ level 2
1	GCSE (grade D-G), Foundation Diploma, BTEC Introductory, OCR level 1 National, Welsh Baccalaureate Foundation Diploma, NVQ level 1
Entry	Entry level certificate/award

The rest of this chapter describes the main qualification routes open to you – whether you decide to continue your learning at school or college, or within the workplace.

Continuing with full-time learning

As discussed in chapter five, the 14-16 curriculum is becoming more flexible, with opportunities to study both work-related and general courses. The post-16 curriculum has also been made more flexible. After year 11, you will be able to take general academic qualifications, learn about a particular area of work, do a mixture of both, or start work-based learning.

Besides deciding on which course to follow, you may also have to choose where to study – to remain at your school (if they have a sixth form and offer the courses you want) or go to college.

Let's look at the main courses and qualifications available.

AS and A levels

The choice of subjects available at advanced subsidiary (AS) and advanced (A) level is similar to that offered at GCSE, but there may be some new subjects, such as psychology or sociology. Each A level is made up of four units. The first two units lead to an AS level qualification, and a further two units make up an A2 – the second half of the A level course. Certain subjects, including music and the sciences, are made up of three units for an AS qualification and six units for an A level. AS and A levels are graded at A-E for pass grades with U grade for unclassified; however, an A* grade is being introduced at A level for those taking exams from 2010.

AS and A levels are also available in applied subjects including travel and tourism, applied art and design and applied ICT. Each subject introduces a broad area of work. A levels in applied subjects can be single awards (which are made up of three units for an AS level, and six units for an A level) or double awards (made up of six units for an AS level, and 12 units for an A level). Some applied subjects are only available as single awards.

If you don't yet know what subjects you want to take at AS/A level, don't worry. There is no need to make up your mind at this stage – in fact, it is not always advisable to make up your mind too early, as your interests are likely to change and develop over the next couple of years. Make sure that you have a broad mix of GCSE subjects, as discussed in chapter five. You can then make the decisions about advanced-level courses during year 11.

Although schools and colleges set their own rules, most normally require you to have gained at least a GCSE grade C (sometimes grade B) in a subject, to allow you to take it at AS/A level. In some subjects, particularly science and languages, the AS level work follows on from GCSE. These are subjects in which you develop your knowledge step by step, and they are obviously more difficult to take up at AS/A level if you have not studied them before.

You should seriously consider keeping your post-16 curriculum broad – perhaps by taking an arts subject at AS if you are doing mainly science subjects, or including an applied A level along with your other A level subjects.

After AS/A levels, you can enter employment or continue onto higher education.

Diplomas

Available in some schools and colleges in England, these new qualifications combine theoretical study with applied and practical learning. They are offered at three levels, all of which may be available post-16:

- Foundation Diploma – a level 1 qualification equivalent to five GCSEs grades D-G

- Higher Diploma – a level 2 qualification equivalent to seven GCSEs grades A*-C

- Advanced Diploma – a level 3 qualification equivalent to three and a half A levels (Progression Diploma – equivalent to two and a half A levels).

From 2011, Extended Diplomas will be available at each Diploma level and in each subject area. These will include more in-depth and independent study, and a greater focus on English and maths.

See chapter seven for more information on Diploma structure and the subjects available.

BTEC courses

BTEC qualifications are awarded by Edexcel. You usually learn about a particular area of work, sometimes a very specific area. Some examples of BTEC courses are mechanical engineering, 3D design, music technology and public services. They are offered mainly by colleges of further education, but some are available in school sixth forms.

BTEC Introductory qualifications

These are level 1 qualifications that provide a practical introduction to an area of work. Introductory Diplomas are made up of eight units and Introductory Certificates are made up of four units.

BTEC First qualifications

A BTEC First Certificate equates to two GCSEs at grades A*-C and a Diploma equates to four GCSEs at grades A*-C. Particular entry qualifications are not usually laid down. If you have a BTEC First qualification, you can progress to another course, or get a job with training.

BTEC National qualifications

BTEC National qualifications are available as:

- a six-unit National Award (equivalent to one A level)

- a 12-unit National Certificate (equivalent to two A levels)

- an 18-unit National Diploma (equivalent to three A levels).

Entry requirements for a BTEC National course are generally four GCSEs at grades A*-C or the equivalent. They can be studied full time or part time. If you have a BTEC National qualification, you can go on to a higher education course or go straight into employment.

National Vocational Qualifications (NVQs)

You can, after year 11, follow a course related to a specific occupation. Programmes leading to NVQs train you in the skills you need to do a particular job – such as hairdressing, administration, catering or horticulture. Over 900 subjects are available. It is possible to do some NVQs at further education colleges, but normally you are observed and assessed whilst at work and need to show that you have the competence to do the job. NVQs are available at five levels.

OCR Nationals

These are worked-related qualifications at levels 1-3, which are available both full and part time. Subjects available at level three include art and design, business, public services and sport. OCR level 3 Nationals include:

- a six-unit Certificate (equivalent to one A level)

- a 12-unit Diploma (equivalent to two A levels)

- an 18-unit Extended Diploma (equivalent to three A levels).

City & Guilds

City & Guilds offers qualifications that relate to specific job areas, at all levels and in subjects ranging from legal work to beauty therapy. Courses are normally available at colleges of further education. Many are taken on a part-time basis.

International Baccalaureate

The International Baccalaureate Diploma is offered by some schools and colleges, and usually takes two years. Students study six subjects as well as completing an extended essay, a unit on the theory of knowledge and taking part in 'creativity, action and service'.

Welsh Baccalaureate

The Welsh Baccalaureate is made up of a core programme of activities including key skills, work-related education and an individual investigation. The Advanced Diploma includes the Core Certificate at Advanced level, plus two A levels, an NVQ level 3 or a BTEC National Certificate or equivalent. More information on the Welsh Baccalaureate, including the Foundation and Intermediate Diploma, can be found in chapter five.

Cambridge Pre-U

This is a new level 3 qualification offered in a limited number of schools and colleges. The Cambridge Pre-U is designed to prepare students for study at university.

Extended Project

The Extended Project is a piece of research, perhaps relating to one of your other subjects or just an area you are interested in. The topic of your project must be agreed with your teacher. You plan and carry out your own research and present your findings either through an essay, a performance, or a piece of creative work. The Extended Project is part of Advanced Diplomas, but can also be taken as a qualification in its own right. It is equivalent in size to an AS level.

GCSEs after year 11

Whether or not you can take GCSEs after the age of 16 can only be answered by individual schools and colleges, according to their arrangements.

Resitting GCSEs

It is always useful to know you can have a second chance, but don't allow it to lull you into a false sense of security. You will need to think carefully why you did not do so well the first time around, and be prepared to work hard. Resitting doesn't automatically mean that you will improve your grades. However, gaining a grade C or above in English and maths can certainly be helpful, and if you feel you can achieve these grades second time around, such subjects may be worth resitting.

Extending your GCSEs

You may decide to choose a subject you haven't studied before. Subjects that might appeal to you could be a new modern foreign language, psychology, sociology or a GCSE in a work-related subject like business or health and social care. Although an applied GCSE gives you a chance to learn about a broad area of work, other qualifications, such as a Diploma or BTEC qualification, may be an alternative.

Learning in the workplace

Getting a job

Instead of staying on in full-time education, you could choose to get a job, possibly through a Government-funded programme, such as an Apprenticeship (described below). If you go for a job, you need to check that you are offered training. It can be very tempting to jump into the first position you are offered because it is available and the money is attractive, but think about your longer-term prospects and where you are aiming.

If you enter employment aged 16 or 17, and have not yet achieved qualifications to level 2 (see the NQF at the beginning of this chapter) you are entitled to **time off for study or training**. This gives you reasonable paid time off during working hours to study or train – at college, in the workplace or elsewhere – for level 2 qualifications. Click on 'Education and learning', then 'It's your choice: options after 16', then 'Skills for work' on: www.directgov.gov.uk

Remember, when you are looking for work, employers want people with transferable skills, enthusiasm and the right attitude. They want employees who are flexible and adaptable, willing to learn, dependable and reliable. So, qualifications are not everything – they just set the minimum educational level required by many employers. And employers are often very flexible – if you haven't got the stated qualifications needed for a job, there may be other qualifications you have gained which are acceptable equivalents.

"I'm training to be a make-up artist. It's a foundation apprenticeship."

Apprenticeships

Apprenticeships offer training based with an employer leading to an NVQ specific to the particular job, attendance at a college or another training provider to take a technical certificate (such as a BTEC qualification), and key/functional skills qualifications (see chapter five). Apprentices are employed and earn a wage. Over a quarter of a million young people are currently training through Apprenticeships, in over 80 occupational areas.

More about Apprenticeships/Advanced Apprenticeships in England can be found on: www.apprenticeships.org.uk

For more information about Foundation Modern Apprenticeships/Modern Apprenticeships in Wales, see: www.elwa.ac.uk

Apprenticeships/Foundation Modern Apprenticeships

These lead to NVQ level 2. Apprenticeships vary in their length, but take at least 12 months. There are normally no set entry requirements, but some employers set their own criteria or require you to sit a test. You can progress to an Advanced Apprenticeship/Modern Apprenticeship.

Advanced Apprenticeships/Modern Apprenticeships

These are for people aiming to become technicians or managers and lead to NVQ level 3. Advanced Apprenticeships/Modern Apprenticeships take at least two years. There are usually no set entry requirements, but employers will want to be sure that you are able to complete the training, so they may ask for some GCSEs (perhaps including maths and English) at grades A*-C or equivalent, or ask you to take certain tests. Advanced Apprenticeships/Modern Apprenticeships can lead to higher education courses, such as an HNC/D or foundation degree.

Entry to Employment (e2e)/Skill Build

Skill Build (in Wales) and e2e (in England) are preparatory training programmes primarily aimed at those aged 16-18 who are not yet ready to enter an Apprenticeship. Skill Build and e2e help to build up your basic and key/functional skills, and sample different areas of work and/or start some specific job training. The programme is tailored to your needs, and you are provided with plenty of support and guidance. Many people progress to an Apprenticeship/Foundation Modern Apprenticeship.

Programme Led Pathways (PLPs)

A PLP is a route into an Apprenticeship if you are not in employment. This might be because a suitable job is not yet available or you are waiting to start a job. Normally, during this time, you attend a college, training centre or work placement and take the technical certificate and/or key skill elements of the Apprenticeship. As soon as you start work, you are transferred to an employed Apprenticeship.

Decisions at age 18+

University – what me?

Thinking about what you might do at 18 probably sounds a long way off. You may feel that continuing your studies beyond A levels (or equivalent qualifications) is carrying learning a bit too far! However, it's not too early to start thinking...

Each year, many young people enter full-time higher education. This means courses beyond level 3 – such as degrees, HNDs and foundation degrees. The Government's aim is for 50% of people aged under 30 – yes, one in every two – to participate in higher education by 2010. And people of all backgrounds are being encouraged to consider it.

Going to university can be one of the best experiences of your life! Why?

- It gives you the chance to spend three years or so finding out more about a subject (or subjects) that really interests you. Just look at a university prospectus or website to see the range of courses available. It's staggering! With so many different courses on offer, how can you not find something which would not only be fascinating to study, but could also lead to an interesting job?

- University gives you the chance to live independently and take responsibility as to how you spend your time, what you do, what you eat and so on.

- The opportunity to get to know people from completely different backgrounds and cultures and to make lots of new friends.

- A higher education qualification opens up lots of career possibilities that would not otherwise be available to you.

The downside? Probably not much money to live on while being a student – but then you will be with others in a similar position, and your future earnings potential should be far more!

A degree course is not usually a training for a career; it is an academic education. Many arts graduates' careers have little connection with their degree subject. A history graduate may enter a marketing training scheme with a large company, for example. They may not use history directly at all, but they would be using skills that they have developed during their degree, like problem solving, researching, analysing and presenting information. Over half of graduate jobs are open to graduates of any subject. So you don't have to be sure of your career direction when choosing your higher education.

For an idea of the range of higher education courses on offer, look at:

- *The Big Guide* – published by the Universities and Colleges Admissions Service (UCAS), or see: www.ucas.ac.uk

- university and college of higher education prospectuses and websites.

The Government is running a campaign called Aimhigher to interest more young people in higher education, especially those from backgrounds where going to university is not the usual pathway. If you get the chance to participate in any activities run through Aimhigher, say yes!

Higher education entry requirements

Exact entry requirements for higher education courses vary between institutions so you should always check prospectuses carefully. However, the minimum entry requirements are as follows.

- For a degree course, you need at least two A levels or equivalent qualifications (see level 3 of the NQF at the beginning of this chapter) plus supporting GCSEs or equivalent (maths and English at grades A*-C are often required). In practice, many universities ask for three A levels.

- For entry to an HNC/HND, you normally need at least one A level (or equivalent), plus supporting GCSEs.

- There are no set entry requirements for foundation degrees – individual institutions set their own criteria; typically they will require an NVQ level 3 or an equivalent qualification.

Many higher education institutions state their entry requirements using the UCAS Tariff, whereby points are awarded for achieving qualifications at different grades. Many qualifications attract Tariff points, including key skills, BTEC Nationals and the International Baccalaureate Diploma – but some universities do not accept certain qualifications for particular degree courses, so it is important to check that the qualification you take will be accepted by universities for the course you are interested in.

Learn while you earn ...

Whatever job you go into, it would be unusual if you didn't keep on learning and training. In most workplaces, the way tasks are carried out and the way systems are organised frequently change due to technological developments, new products and services, the amalgamation of departments or whole companies, and all sorts of other reasons. In fact, if things didn't change, it would get very boring!

Many people who enter employment carry on gaining qualifications through part-time study. Just because you start work at a young age doesn't mean that you can't get a degree. If continuing to higher education as a full-time student doesn't appeal or would be difficult, there are more and more opportunities to continue to learn while in a job.

- The Open University, and similar providers, offers the opportunity to do a wide range of courses.

- Many higher education courses, e.g. foundation degrees, can be studied part time, e.g. through day release or by distance learning.

- Many bodies offer professional qualifications in their own field which are equivalent to degree level and beyond.

- NVQs can be gained in the workplace up to level 5.

The future of work

The workplace has changed dramatically since your grandparents' or even parents' day. Try talking to them about their first jobs! And jobs continue to change: it's not that long ago that there were no website designers or sports psychologists.

- Most jobs are for qualified and skilled people, so it's really important to gain the highest level of qualifications that you can, or your choices will be limited.

- Employers' needs are changing. A government report recently found that more and more employers need staff with higher levels of skill to deal with the increasing use of technology.

- Ways of working have become more flexible - apart from doing full-time or part-time jobs, you could job share, work from home for all or part of your time, or work during term time only. Often jobs are available on a fixed-term basis - for one, two or three years, for example. Some people use their skills to work freelance - undertaking work for different employers.

- You are more likely to change your job, and possibly your career, than your parents or grandparents did.

- There are currently skill shortages in certain employment areas. Labour market information can be found on: www.statistics.gov.uk

A final word...

If all the talk of qualifications and courses after 16 seems a bit confusing, don't worry. You've plenty of time to explore the various options before you need to make a decision, and there will be lots of help available. If you want to find out more, the options after year 11 are discussed more fully in *Decisions at 15/16+*, which is a companion book to this one.

Chapter nine

Making the choice

What subjects do I need for the future?

It's one thing to know which subjects are important for a particular career and quite another to act on that knowledge. 'What do I need?' is a question you can answer only after taking all the relevant facts into consideration. A good starting point is your career plan as it stands now, however sketchy it may be.

Career plan checklist

If you have a definite career plan ...

- Have you checked what subjects you need for your chosen career? If not, consult the careers guide in part three of this book.

- Is it likely that you will achieve these subjects at the right level and grade? If the answer is definitely not, perhaps you should consider alternative careers.

Think about what is really triggering your likes and dislikes.

What am I good at?

Are you good at the things you like? Do you always like the things you are good at? How soon should you specialise in your best subjects? Can this be carried too far? Could you drop some of your good subjects for two years and then take them up again? What makes you good at a subject anyway, e.g. do you have particular skills?

What is recommended?

Who recommends you to do what? What do your teachers suggest you do? Have your parents or other members of your family had their say? Are your teachers and family giving you conflicting advice? How can you sort out whose opinions are right for you?

What do I need?

How far ahead have you looked? Does your choice allow you sufficient flexibility? What changes might occur in the career field that interests you? If changes come, will you be able to adapt to them? Where can you get advice on questions like these?

How many subjects should I take?

It is difficult to generalise as everyone is different. The National Curriculum dictates that you must take exams in some subjects, and your school's timetabling policy may also impose other restrictions – ask your teachers.

As far as subjects outside the compulsory National Curriculum are concerned, take as many as you can without overstretching yourself. As you may not achieve all the grades you hope for, it is a good idea to take more subjects than you need, but don't go to extremes. It may be better to achieve six GCSEs with good grades rather than ten with low grades.

Resolving clashes

If you are forced into a choice you are not happy about, think of ways of getting around the clash.

- If you can't take an ICT course, could you teach yourself at home using online learning packages?

- If another subject clashes with music, could you try private lessons or set up your own band?

- If drama isn't possible, how about auditioning for the next school play or joining your local amateur dramatics society?

- If it isn't possible to take a specific language at school, could someone who speaks the language fluently help you informally, or in the future, could you take an evening class?

Some subjects at GCSE are offered again in the sixth form or at further education colleges. Others can be bypassed at GCSE but still studied to AS or A level. There is often more flexibility than first appears. Just because you don't take a subject at GCSE doesn't necessarily mean you can never study it again!

Making the choice

Now comes the crunch. After all the reading, talking, finding out and discussion, the choice has to be made. And only **you** can make it. You have the information you need; now you just have to draw it all together.

To help you make decisions, you could make a chart.

1. Across the top of a large piece of paper, write a list of all the subjects you can choose from.

2. Down the left-hand side of the paper, write down the following 'criteria':

    - I enjoy it

    - I am good at it

    - it is recommended

    - I need it for the future.

For each subject, put a tick besides all the criteria that apply. For instance, if you have written art and design, put a tick in the relevant box if you enjoy it, if you need it for the future etc. When you've finished your chart, the pattern of ticks, and total number for each subject, may help you make your decision.

Sometimes, making a list of your options, and the pros and cons of each, can really help you to see things more clearly.

Chapter ten

How to find out more

Getting help

No one pretends that it's easy making decisions about your future, that's why getting help is important. Remember that people may have different points of view, but ultimately, decisions have to be your own.

N.B. The inclusion of a book or website in this chapter does not, in any way, endorse the quality or accuracy of its content. Where possible, check how recently factual information has been updated.

Who can help you with your choices?

- Your form teacher or tutor – they know you in an all-round school situation.

- Your personal/careers adviser and careers teacher – they will be able to give you unbiased advice on the choices you will have to make.

- Your subject teachers can offer a realistic view of your ability in their subject and whether you would benefit from taking the subject further.

- College staff can advise you on routes through further education.

- People you know who work in any careers you are interested in – although bear in mind that entry routes may have changed since they were at school!

- Your parents/carer, family and friends, who know you best of all as a person.

Help with problems and concerns

If there are things happening in your life which make it difficult to study – such as bullying, problems with your family or health concerns – your Connexions personal adviser (if you have one) or your form tutor can help you to talk things through. Some schools have student counsellors who are trained to help in just these sorts of situations. Otherwise, perhaps you could discuss the issue with another responsible person.

There are also websites and telephone helplines you can try. Below are a few examples.

- To talk to someone with complete confidentiality about problems, call Childline: 0800 1111. You can also find advice and information on just about any topic on: **www.childline.org.uk**

- If you have a problem which concerns your legal rights, ring the **Children's Legal Centre**: 0800 783 2187.

- If problems are making you feel depressed, stressed or angry, try: **www.youngminds.org.uk**

- If you are upset because your parents are splitting up, have a look at: **www.itsnotyourfault.org**

- For help with revision and study skills: **www.bbc.co.uk/schools**

- Other sites offering advice on many topics which affect young people include:

www.connexions-direct.com (tel: 080 800 13 2 19)

www.youthinformation.com

www.need2know.co.uk

www.thesite.org.uk

www.bbc.co.uk/onelife

www.kidscape.org.uk (helpline: 08451 205 204)

Finding out more about careers

There's lots of information out there to help you make learning and career choices.

Printed careers materials

After most of the job areas in the careers guide, books have been recommended. The prices quoted do not usually include postage and packing. Remember that many of the resources will be available for reference in your school or Connexions/careers centre library. The following are just a few of the many publications that you may find useful, some of which have been referred to in the careers guide.

Booklets

These booklets are published by DCSF Publications. You should get copies of them at school, but they can also be downloaded or used interactively on: **www.connexions-direct.com**

- *Which Way Now?* – information on choices in year 9
- *It's Your Choice* – provides year 10 and 11 students with information about further education, training and employment options.

Course reference books

Directory of Vocational and Further Education 2008/2009 – a complete guide to further education courses in the UK. Published by Pearson Education.

Big Guide – published by UCAS (with accompanying CD-ROM). Gives details of all full-time higher education courses in the UK.

Directory of Teacher Training Courses 2009 – lists undergraduate and postgraduate teacher training courses. Published by Trotman.

Progression to... series published by UCAS, £15.99 each. Covers some of the most competitive degree courses, such as engineering, maths, psychology and law, and includes advice on applying and job prospects.

Careers guides

Decisions at 15/16+ – published in association with CRAC by Lifetime Publishing, £11.99.

A-Z of Careers and Jobs – published by Kogan Page, £14.99.

Working in... series published by VT Lifeskills, £8.50 each. Contain profiles of people working in a wide range of careers.

How to Get Ahead in... series – published by Heinemann, £8.50 each.

Careers and Jobs in... series – published by Kogan Page, £7.99 each.

Careers Uncovered... series – published by Trotman, £11.99/£12.99 each.

Real Life Guides... series – published by Trotman, £9.99 each.

The Into... careers series – published by Skill (National Bureau for Students with Disabilities), £6.50 each or £2.50 for disabled students.

Useful websites

Over the past few years, an amazing number of websites have become available which offer all kinds of information to help you choose courses, qualifications and a career. A few useful websites are listed below; many of the sites give information on more than one topic.

For careers advice and information on jobs and careers

If you are aged 13 to 19 and live in England, you can get advice and information on choices related to learning, careers and lifestyle issues. Tel: 080 800 13 2 19, or see: **www.connexions-direct.com**

Part of the Connexions website, Jobs 4U has hundreds of detailed career profiles and case studies: **www.connexions-direct.com/jobs4u**

For help with all sorts of learning and careers issues, tel: 0800 100 900 or see: **www.learndirect-advice.co.uk**

Click on 'jobs and careers' for careers advice, information on public sector jobs, voluntary work and government-funded training programmes: **www.direct.gov.uk/employment**

For information on education, training and employment in Wales: **www.careerswales.com**

The National Information and Advice Service for young people aged 11 to 25 in Wales: **www.cliconline.co.uk**

Although aimed at graduates, there's lots of information about different careers, entry routes and case studies: **www.prospects.ac.uk**

Provides career information and advice and has links to specific occupational websites: **www.careers-gateway.co.uk**

If you register on the website, you can download the Inside Careers guides, which cover a range of careers: **www.insidecareers.co.uk**

For information on learning opportunities

For all kinds of information on education, learning, qualifications, choices etc: **www.direct.gov.uk/en/educationandlearning**

For more information on the 14-19 curriculum and qualifications, see:

- **http://curriculum.qca.org** (National Curriculum in England)
- **http://wales.gov.uk/topics/educationandskills** (National Curriculum in Wales)
- **www.dcsf.gov.uk/14-19**
- **www.dcsf.gov.uk/qualifications**
- **http://yp.direct.gov.uk/diplomas** (for information on Diplomas in England).

For information on qualifications offered through the main awarding bodies/exam board, see:

- **www.aqa.org.uk** (Assessment and Qualifications Alliance)
- **www.ccea.org.uk** (Council for the Curriculum, Examinations and Assessment – Northern Ireland)
- **www.cityandguilds.com** (City & Guilds)
- **www.edexcel.org.uk** and **www.examzone.co.uk** (Edexcel)
- **www.ocr.org.uk** (Oxford, Cambridge and RSA)
- **www.wjec.co.uk** (WJEC – previously known as the Welsh Joint Education Committee).

The 14-19 areawide prospectus helps you find local learning opportunities if you live in England: **www.futures4me.co.uk**

To find a course and information about taking specifically-designed learndirect courses, tel: 0800 100 900, or see: **www.learndirect-advice.co.uk**

For information on Apprenticeships: **www.apprenticeships.org.uk**

To search for all types of post-16 courses and for information about hundreds of different careers: **www.hotcourses.com**

Universities and Colleges Admissions Service – has a higher education course-search facility: **www.ucas.com**

For all kinds of information on higher education courses, finance and student life: **www.aimhigher.ac.uk**

A website on foundation degrees; includes a course search facility: **www.fdf.ac.uk**

A gateway site to the UK's universities, colleges and research organisations: **www.hero.ac.uk**

Skill – the National Bureau for Students with Disabilities – a charity promoting opportunities for people with disabilities in post-16 education, training and employment: **www.skill.org.uk**

Information on studying (and working) in Europe: **www.careerseurope.co.uk**

Computer-based careers resources

There is a range of computer-based resources which can both help you to generate ideas about future careers and provide detailed information on these. Ask your personal adviser/careers tutor for advice on using the computer programs and CD-ROMs which may be available to you. Many careers software programs are now available online.

Computer-based careers resources include:

- *KeyCLIPS* – information on careers, training and education, subject choices etc; the online version is called eCLIPS

- *Job Explorer Database* – a Careersoft multimedia resource with a database of job profiles

- *Fast Tomato* – an interactive careers guidance system from the Morrisby Organisation

- *Kudos* – from Cascaid, generates ideas for careers based on questions about yourself

- *Careerscape Online* – from Cascaid, includes information on higher education courses, careers and labour market statistics.

Publishers' contact details

There are many publishers that produce resources (some of which are listed in this chapter) to help you to make decisions about your future learning and career. A few of the main publishers are listed here, together with their contact details. They may be able to send you a copy of their current catalogue.

Heinemann
Tel: 01865 888000
Email: enquiries@pearson.com
www.heinemann.co.uk

How To Books
Tel: 01865 375794
Email: info@howtobooks.co.uk
www.howtobooks.co.uk

Kogan Page
Tel: 020 7278 0433; 01903 828800 (sales)
Email: kpsales@kogan-page.com
www.kogan-page.com

Lifetime Publishing
Tel: 01225 716023; 01202 665432 (orders)
Email: sales@lifetime-publishing.co.uk
www.lifetime-publishing.co.uk

Pearson Education
Tel 870 607 3777
www.pearsoned.co.uk

Skill: National Bureau for Students with Disabilities
Tel: 020 7450 0620.
Email: info@skill.org.uk
www.skill.org.uk

Trotman
Tel: 0870 900 2665 (orders and customer service)
Email: orders@trotman.co.uk
www.trotman.co.uk

Universities and Colleges Admissions Service (UCAS)
Tel: 01242 544610 (publications)
Email: publicationservices@ucas.ac.uk
www.ucasbooks.com

VT Lifeskills
Tel: 01329 229138
Email: sales@vtlifeskills.co.uk
www.vtlifeskills.co.uk

Part three
Careers guide

Careers guide

Introduction

This section is a guide to careers. A wide range of career areas (although by no means all of them!) is described, together with addresses, websites and books to help you find out more. An index of career areas is provided at the back of the book.

Course entry requirements

For each career area in the guide, there may be more than one entry route. For instance, it may be possible for someone with relevant experience to enter a career with fewer qualifications than those stated. Entry requirements are constantly changing, so check with individual course providers and professional bodies.

In the careers guide, you will be told what qualifications are appropriate to enter the career area that interests you. Below is a summary of the usual entry requirements. More detailed information is available in chapter eight. **It is essential that you check individual course/programme entry requirements carefully.**

Entry requirements for advanced-level courses

For entry to most advanced-level courses, such as A levels, BTEC National and Advanced Diploma courses, you normally need at least four GCSEs at grades A*-C. Your school or college will advise you.

For certain subjects, you must have a grounding in the subject at GCSE level. For instance, you can normally only take French AS/A level if you have a good pass in GCSE French. For other subjects, such as psychology or economics, you don't need to have previously studied the subject.

Entry requirements for Apprenticeships

Entry requirements vary but you will need to show that you are capable of studying at the required level. For some Advanced Apprenticeships/Modern Apprenticeships employers may ask for particular GCSEs at grades A*-C.

Entry requirements for higher education courses

For entry to a degree course, you normally need at least two A levels or equivalent qualifications, plus supporting GCSEs or equivalent. There are no set entry requirements for foundation degrees; individual institutions set their own criteria. Entry to a Higher National course is usually possible with at least one A level or equivalent qualification. Many universities express their requirements for higher education courses using UCAS Tariff points.

Using careers libraries

Once you have read about a career area in this book, you may want to find out more. You can contact the bodies listed, read the books recommended or visit the websites given. In addition, your Connexions/careers library will have more information.

The Connexions Resource Centre Index (CRCI) helps you to find information on careers grouped into occupational areas.

No idea where to start?

If you are not yet sure what kind of career you want, the following lists may give you just a few ideas about the job areas that might interest you.

Examples of jobs which involve working with people, often in a helping or caring capacity:

- advisory work
- ambulance service work
- complementary medicine
- early years childcare and education
- nursing
- prison work
- psychology
- public relations
- social work
- teaching
- travel and tourism work
- youth and community work.

Examples of jobs which involve active and/or outdoor work:

- Armed Forces (Army, Royal Air Force, and Royal Navy and Royal Marines)
- building crafts (such as carpentry, plumbing or roofing)
- engineering
- environmental work
- farming and agricultural advisory work
- firefighting
- forestry
- horses – careers with
- police and security services

- sports and fitness instructing
- veterinary work
- wastes management.

Examples of jobs which involve practical work:

- beauty therapy and consultancy
- building services engineering
- chiropractic and osteopathy
- dentistry
- fashion – clothing production
- hairdressing
- horticulture
- laboratory technician work
- motor vehicle work
- occupational therapy
- physiotherapy
- podiatry.

Examples of jobs which involve maths and/or science:

- actuarial work
- architecture
- astronomy and space science
- biomedical science
- economics
- financial advice
- food science and technology
- forensic science
- materials science and metallurgy
- medicine and surgery
- pharmacy
- statistics.

Examples of jobs which involve administrative and clerical work:

- accountancy
- banking and building society work
- Civil Service
- company secretarial work
- insurance
- library and information science and management
- local government administration
- logistics and transport
- management
- medical administration work
- purchasing and stock control
- secretarial work.

Examples of jobs which involve creative and/or media work:

- advertising
- animation
- art and design (such as painters, designers and craftspeople who make jewellery, pottery or carvings)
- media: radio, TV, film and video/DVD
- creative therapies
- dancing
- drama
- journalism
- marketing
- music
- photography
- publishing.

Careers guide A-Z

Accountancy

Accountants prepare or audit the financial accounts of an organisation, and give advice on important matters such as tax and management systems. Accountants need to be very organised and efficient. They work in the public sector, in commercial companies of all types and sizes and in firms of accountants. It's possible to specialise in a particular area of work. Many accountants move into general management, or even become directors.

Accounting technicians work as support staff to accountants in many different roles. They may take on considerable responsibility, especially in smaller organisations.

Getting started

- You can gain the qualifications of the different accountancy professional bodies, the biggest of which are listed below, through full- or part-time study or distance learning.

- Most entrants to **accountancy** training have degrees, but you could start with GCSEs at grades A*-C, including English and maths, plus two A levels and work your way up.

- You can train as an **accounting technician** without any formal academic entry requirements, but certain qualifications may exempt you from some stages of training. Qualifications are offered by the AAT and ACCA (see below). Qualified accounting technicians may be exempt from parts of accountancy training.

- Apprenticeships and Advanced Apprenticeships in accounting offer young people training with an employer and lead to NVQ levels 2 and 3 respectively.

- If you are interested in accountancy, Diplomas in business, administration and finance are being introduced from 2009.

Find out more

Association of Accounting Technicians (AAT)
140 Aldersgate Street, London EC1A 4HY.
Tel: 0845 863 0800. www.aat.org.uk

Association of Chartered Certified Accountants (ACCA)
ACCA Connect, 2 Central Quay, 89 Hydepark Street, Glasgow G3 8BW.
Tel: 0141 582 2000. www.accaglobal.com

Chartered Institute of Management Accountants
26 Chapter Street, London SW1P 4NP.
Tel: 020 8849 2251. www.cimaglobal.com

The Chartered Institute of Public Finance and Accountancy
3 Robert Street, London WC2N 6RL.
Tel: 020 7543 5600. www.cipfa.org.uk

The Institute of Chartered Accountants in England and Wales
Gloucester House, 399 Silbury Boulevard, Central Milton Keynes MK9 2HL.
Tel: 01908 248040. www.icaew.co.uk/careers

Acting: see Drama

Actuarial work

Actuaries are highly-skilled (and highly-paid) mathematicians. They use statistics, such as the life expectancy of different groups, to calculate life assurance premiums and payouts and design pension schemes and other financial products. Actuaries also work for business and government to make financial predictions and recommend courses of action.

Getting started

- For entry to actuarial training, you normally need a degree in actuarial science, maths, economics or statistics, or another subject with a high maths content. If you have maths A level at grade A-C, a degree in any subject is acceptable.

- Entry to training directly after A levels is unusual, but it is possible with three GCSEs at grades A*-C, including English, plus an A level in a mathematical subject at grade A or B and another A level at grade A-C.

- It normally takes a graduate entrant five years to qualify; A level entrants take longer. All trainees study for professional exams while working in an actuary's office.

Find out more

Institute of Actuaries
Napier House, 4 Worcester Street, Oxford OX1 2AW.
Tel: 01865 268200. www.actuaries.org.uk

Acupuncture: see Complementary medicine

Administrative work: see Civil Service, Local government administration, Secretarial work

---

Advertising

Advertising involves promoting products or services through the print and broadcast media. It's a highly competitive business, often seen as glamorous. Determination, good communication skills and creativity are needed whatever the job. **Copywriters** produce the words to go with the visual images provided by **artists**, **film crew** or **photographers**, and **account executives** liaise between the creative team and the client.

Getting started

- You're more likely to get into advertising if you have a higher education qualification. There are specialist courses which prepare you for work in advertising, but there are also opportunities for graduates of any subject. Some advertising agencies offer graduate training schemes.

- You'll also need evidence of a creative imagination, combined with business sense.

- Once employed, you can apply to take the professional exams of CAM (see below).

- To work on the creative side, you are likely to need a qualification or background in a relevant subject, such as graphic design, photography or film.

- If you are interested in a career in advertising, Diplomas in creative and media may be available.

Find out more

Advertising Association

7th Floor North, Artillery House, 11-19 Artillery Row, London SW1P 1RT. Tel: 020 7340 1100. www.adassoc.org.uk

Getting into Advertising is available on the Association's website.

CAM (Communication, Advertising & Marketing Education Foundation)

Moor Hall, Cookham, Maidenhead, Berkshire SL6 9QH. Tel: 01628 427120. www.camfoundation.com

Working in Marketing, Advertising & PR – published by VT Lifeskills, £8.50.

Advisory work

All kinds of people are employed to give advice on specific issues – there are fire prevention officers, financial advisers, life coaches, legal advice centre workers, Connexions personal advisers, health visitors and consumer and welfare rights advisers to name just a few. Many of these jobs are in the public and voluntary sectors. Some advisory jobs also involve mediation (helping people to come to an agreement) and/or advocacy (representing or speaking for other people).

Getting started

- Advisory work is often a career for people with some experience.

- Some of these jobs will need a relevant degree or professional qualification; others can be entered with a good general education.

- You need excellent communication skills – most importantly the ability to listen – as well as a thorough knowledge of your subject area.

- Think about which area of work you are interested in, and the kind of clients you wish to help. Once you've narrowed down your choices, look in your Connexions/careers library for information on entry requirements and training.

Find out more

Working in Advice & Counselling – published by VT Lifeskills, £8.50.

Aeronautical engineering: see Engineering

Agricultural work: see Farming and agricultural advisory work

Air cabin crew

Air cabin crew look after passengers on board a plane – they make sure customers are as comfortable as possible, serve meals and drinks and sell merchandise. Some passengers may be nervous or demanding. Passenger safety is a priority, and, in emergencies, it is the responsibility of the cabin crew to ensure the safe evacuation of the plane.

Getting started

- Cabin crew are normally recruited from the age of 18; many candidates have had another job before they apply, perhaps dealing with people.

- A good general education is required – some GCSEs are usually expected, including English and maths at grades A*-C. Other useful subjects include foreign languages, geography, leisure and tourism and health and social care. Diplomas in travel and tourism are being introduced from 2009.

- You need to be physically fit and may have to pass a medical examination. The height requirement is normally between 5'2"/157cm and 6'2"/188cm.

- You need to have a friendly, reassuring and approachable manner, work well in a team, have good communication skills, a smart appearance and the ability to handle difficult situations.

- Training starts with a course lasting several weeks at a training centre.

Find out more

Contact individual airlines to find out about their entry requirements.

Air Force: see Royal Air Force

Air traffic control

Air traffic controllers direct the take off, landing and movement of air traffic by giving radio messages to pilots. They keep track of the movement of aircraft using radar and computer systems. Most work at the main area control centres near Portsmouth, Heathrow and Glasgow and in Manchester. Others work at individual airports.

To work as an air traffic controller, you need good powers of concentration and to be able to keep cool under pressure.

Getting started

- You need to be aged at least 18 when you apply.

- Five GCSEs at grades A*-C, including English and maths, or equivalent, are required.

- You must be eligible to work in the UK.

- A good standard of health, good hearing and eyesight and normal colour vision are needed. You can wear glasses or contact lenses, but within certain prescription limits.

- Initial training takes from six to 12 months at a specially-designed training centre in Bournemouth. You are then posted to an operational unit for further training of up to two years.

Find out more

NATS

Recruitment and Selection Centre, Corporate and Technical Centre, 4000 Parkway, Whiteley, Fareham, Hampshire PO15 7FL.
Tel: 01489 616090. www.natscareers.co.uk

Airbroking: see Logistics and transport

Alexander technique: see Complementary medicine

Ambulance service work

Ambulance services are divided into the Patient Transport Service and the Accident and Emergency Service. **Ambulance care assistants** work in the Patient Transport Service, taking people who cannot drive themselves, or cannot use public transport, to hospitals and clinics. Most of their clients are older people or recovering from injury. **Ambulance technicians** work alongside paramedics in the Accident and Emergency Service and are trained to give initial medical aid before transporting sick or injured people to hospital. **Ambulance paramedics** are able to use more advanced medical procedures and the latest life-saving equipment. Some ambulance services use helicopters and motorbikes to get to patients quickly. **Emergency care practitioners** may be based in a GP surgery, hospital accident and emergency department or in the community. They assess patients, provide treatment and prescribe medication.

Getting started

- **Ambulance care assistants** need a good general education – GCSEs or equivalent qualifications may be expected. Training lasts for two to three weeks.

- **Technicians** may need some GCSEs at grades A*-C (or equivalent) including English, maths and a science. They have to pass a series of tests. Training lasts for around 12 weeks.

- By law, **paramedics** must be registered by the Health Professions Council having completed an approved course. Paramedics may be experienced technicians who undergo further training and exams or, they may hold an approved higher education qualification. Entrants undertake further training in life-saving techniques.

- **Emergency care practitioners** are experienced paramedics or nurses who have undertaken extra training.

- You need to be physically fit, and to have a full, clean driving licence. Preference may be given to candidates with GCSEs. In some areas, four or five GCSEs at grades A*-C, including English and maths, are required.

- Personal qualities are important: you need to be good with people and able to stay calm in a crisis.

- If you are interested in a career with the ambulance service, Diplomas in public services are being introduced from 2010.

Find out more

Contact your local **Ambulance Service NHS Trust**. You'll find the address in the telephone directory.

The British Paramedic Association
28 Wilfred Street, Derby DE23 8GF.
Tel: 01332 746356. www.britishparamedic.org

Health Professions Council
Park House, 184 Kennington Road, London SE11 4BU.
Tel: 020 7582 0866. www.hpc-uk.org
Website gives details of standards and approved courses.

Working in Community Healthcare – published by VT Lifeskills, £8.50.
Includes a profile of an ambulance care assistant.

Animal keeping: see Zookeeping

Animation

Traditional animation involves drawing or modelling thousands of separate images which, when filmed, give the impression of movement. Nowadays, most animation is done by computer, although it still takes a creative human being to have the original ideas! Animation is used in feature films, adverts, computer games, websites and television programmes. Many animators work for themselves on a freelance basis.

Getting started

- You'll need technical and ICT skills as well as artistic ability.

- Aim to do well in art at GCSE, or equivalent.

- Most successful animators have studied the subject on its own or as part of an art and design higher education course.

- If you are interested in a career in animation, Diplomas in creative and media may be available.

Find out more

Skillset

Focus Point, 21 Caledonian Road, London N1 9GB. The Sector Skills Council for the audio-visual industries.
Tel: 020 7713 9800. Media careers helpline: 08080 300 900.
www.skillset.org/animation/careers

BFI (British Film Institute)

Animation Department, National Film Theatre/BFI, South Bank, Waterloo, London SE1 8XT.
Tel: 020 7815 1329. www.bfi.org.uk

Media Uncovered – published by Trotman, £11.99.

Archaeology

Archaeologists don't just look for buried treasures. A true archaeologist will be as excited about finding the remains of a wooden post or an unfinished mediaeval meal as about finding a golden ornament. Some of the work is done in the field, on excavations, while some involves conservation methods and computer analysis. Work sometimes has to be done very quickly, as an excavation site may only be made available for a few weeks before it's built over.

Getting started

- Your best chance of becoming a professional archaeologist is to study archaeology at university. Some degree courses require science A levels. Useful GCSEs include English, maths, sciences, languages, history and geography.

- There are more archaeology graduates than there are jobs for them to fill, so you will need to be very persistent to find permanent work. Find out where your local digs are and volunteer your services.

- You could always keep archaeology as a very rewarding hobby, and use your degree in archaeology as an entry route to many other careers.

Find out more

Council for British Archaeology (CBA)

St Mary's House, 66 Bootham, York YO30 7BZ.
Tel: 01904 671417. www.britarch.ac.uk
Website has various factsheets on training and careers in archaeology.
The CBA can help would-be volunteers find suitable excavations. It also
runs the Young Archaeologists' Club for young people up to the age of
16.

Working in Cultural Heritage – published by VT Lifeskills, £8.50. Includes
a profile of an archaeologist.

Architecture

Architecture is a mixture of art and science. **Architects** design new
buildings and extend or alter existing buildings. They must understand
the technical side of construction work as well as having artistic ability.
Architects have to work with their clients, with planning authorities and
with building contractors, so they need good communication skills too.
Site visits are part of the job.

Architectural technologists work closely with architects and other
members of the building team. Their work may involve preparing working
drawings, conducting surveys, collecting information, inspecting work at
building sites and responsibility for project management.

There are also posts for **architectural technicians**, who assist
technologists and architects.

Getting started

- It will take you at least seven years to qualify and register as
an **architect**, including time spent at university and in the
workplace gaining practical experience.

- To get on an architecture degree course, your GCSEs will have
to include English, maths and science at grades A*-C, and you
will need at least two A levels or equivalent. The RIBA (see
below) recommends a mixture of arts and science subjects.

- You don't need a qualification in art, but you should be able to
draw and sketch freehand. You may need a portfolio of work to
show your artistic ability.

- **Architectural technologists** can start with good GCSEs or A levels or equivalent, and study for higher qualifications while working. Useful GCSE subjects include English, maths, science, design and technology and ICT. Another route is to study full time at higher education level before entry.

- If you are interested in a career in architecture, Diplomas in construction and the built environment may be available.

Find out more

Royal Institute of British Architects (RIBA)
66 Portland Place, London WIB 4AD.
Tel: 020 7580 5533. www.architecture.com

Chartered Institute of Architectural Technologists (CIAT)
397 City Road, London ECIV INH.
Tel: 020 7278 2206. www.ciat.org.uk
Your Career in Architectural Technology handbook is available on request or can be downloaded from the CIAT's website.

Working in the Built Environment & Construction – published by VT Lifeskills, £8.50. Includes a profile of a trainee architect.

Archive work

Archivists maintain collections of documents and other records – such as film, audiotape, photos, maps and even computer disks – in archives run by local authorities, central government, and a variety of private and commercial organisations. **Archive conservators** repair damaged documents.

Getting started

- **Archivists** need to gain a degree in any subject, followed by a postgraduate course in archives and records management. GCSEs at grades A*-C in subjects such as history, geography and languages are useful.

- To be an **archive conservator** you will need to take a specialist course in archive or paper conservation. Some records offices offer places on the Society of Archivists' Conservation Training Scheme. At GCSE level, chemistry is very important for conservation work.

Find out more

Society of Archivists

Prioryfield House, 20 Canon Street, Taunton, Somerset TA1 1SW.
Tel: 01823 327030. www.archives.org.uk

Working in Cultural Heritage – published by VT Lifeskills, £8.50. Includes a profile of an archivist.

Army

National defence is the main task of all branches of the Forces; they also take part in UN and NATO operations. Today's Army is trained in the latest sophisticated weapons, equipment and management techniques.

There are over 100 specialist roles in the Army, but whatever the specific trade or skill, entrants are first and foremost soldiers, with all the risks that can involve. Army discipline can be pretty tough, during and after training! Women can compete on equal terms with men in all jobs except for those in the Infantry, the Royal Armoured Corps and the Household Cavalry.

Getting started

- Everyone has to pass medical and physical fitness tests and meet nationality requirements.

- You can join the Army as a **soldier** entrant straight from school at 16 without academic qualifications, but if you want to apply for certain jobs, you will need some GCSEs, especially English, maths, science and technology subjects.

- Students at the Army Foundation College in Harrogate are paid a wage while they train. You need to apply in year 11.

- When you learn a trade, you usually work towards nationally-recognised qualifications, such as NVQs. These can be useful in civilian life when you leave the Army.

- To train as an **officer**, the minimum entry qualifications are 180 UCAS Tariff points at AS/A level, or the equivalent, together with 35 ALIS points for your best seven GCSEs (advisers in the Army Careers Information Office can explain this to you), which must include maths, English and either a science or foreign language. However, most entrants to officer training are graduates.

- Some sponsorship and bursary schemes are available to help support selected students through their sixth-form and university studies.
- If you are interested in joining the Armed Forces, Diplomas in public services are being introduced from 2010.

Find out more

Visit your nearest **Armed Forces Careers Office** (Army) or **Army Careers Information Office** (tel: 08457 300 111 if you have difficulty contacting them). A range of careers booklets is available from the offices which will help you to find out about the full range of opportunities. You can also view information on: www.armyjobs.mod.uk

The Armed Forces – from the *Real Life Guides* series – published by Trotman, £9.99.

How to Get Ahead in the Armed Forces – published by Heinemann, £12.99.

Aromatherapy: see Complementary medicine

Art and design

Artists who make a full-time living by producing sculpture, paintings, illustrations etc are few and far between. **Craftspeople**, such as silversmiths, potters, woodcarvers and weavers also produce work of an individual quality. **Designers** apply their creative ability to develop a wide range of products. Some designers work as part of a team for the mass production of articles such as furniture, ceramics, electrical equipment, clothing, fashion and textiles. There are also careers for designers in display and exhibition work and graphic design. Other areas of work include animation, cartoon art, computer art and a wealth of opportunities in the media and communications industry.

Getting started

- Whatever route you take, you will need a really impressive portfolio of artwork to show to college admissions tutors or employers. Obviously, you should aim to take art and design or applied art and design at GCSE.

- Some jobs may be available to people with an A level in art and design or applied art and design, or a relevant BTEC National qualification, but the most interesting opportunities are for graduates. Some people manage to make a living through arts and crafts without formal qualifications, but this is not recommended!

- Most people take a one-year art and design Foundation diploma course before studying for a degree. This course will help you to decide on an area in which you would like to specialise and will allow you to build up a portfolio of work.

- Alternatively, you may be able to enter a degree course directly after taking a BTEC National qualification or A level in applied art and design.

- Degree courses in art and design usually last three years. You can specialise in subjects like graphic design, three-dimensional design, fine art, textile design, multimedia design, animation or fashion design.

- Other higher education routes are HND and foundation degree courses, available in various art and design subject areas.

- Vocational courses, such as those leading to City & Guilds qualifications, are available in a wide variety of art and design subjects – entrance requirements vary.

- Some 14- to 16-year-olds may have the opportunity to take a Young Apprenticeship in art and design, combining learning and work experience with an employer with study at school and college.

- If you are interested in a career in art and design, Diplomas in creative and media may be available.

Find out more

Visit the end-of-year exhibitions of art and design students' work.

National Society for Education in Art and Design
The Gatehouse, Corsham Court, Corsham, Wiltshire SN13 0BZ.
Tel: 01249 714825. www.nsead.org

Working in Art & Design and *Working in Creative & Media* – both published by VT Lifeskills, £8.50 each.

Art & Design Uncovered – published by Trotman, £11.99.

Art therapy: see Creative therapies

Astronomy and space science

Astronomers and space scientists study the planets, stars, galaxies and nebulae, using their knowledge of maths, physics and chemistry to explain their observations. Actual 'star-gazing' forms a very small part of the work. Instead, astronomers and space scientists work on information that is collected for them by satellites, remote telescopes in places with clear skies – like Hawaii, Chile and Australia – and by other recording instruments.

Getting started

- You'll need a degree in physics, maths, astronomy, astrophysics or space science – although chemistry, geology, computer science or electronics can also be useful. You can specialise in astronomy after you graduate, through a postgraduate course.

- You should aim for good A level grades in mathematical subjects and physics, or equivalent qualifications, which means getting good GCSEs in those subjects first!

Find out more

Royal Astronomical Society
Burlington House, Piccadilly, London W1J 0BQ.
Tel: 020 7734 4582. www.ras.org.uk
Produces careers information for school-leavers.

Working in Science – published by VT Lifeskills, £8.50. Includes a profile of an astrophysicist.

Careers with a Science Degree – published by Lifetime Publishing, £11.99.

Auctioneering: see Estate agency, auctioneering and valuation

Audiology technician work: see Medical technology

Banking and building society work

Banks and building societies offer different types of accounts so that we can save money and spend it! They also give advice on investments, lend money to people who want to buy their homes through a mortgage, deal with foreign trade, and assist businesses with their finances. The Government requires people to be qualified before giving advice on investments, pensions etc, so there are special examinations dealing with these areas.

Getting started

- For most jobs in **customer services**, you'll need four GCSEs at grades A*-C, including English and maths.

- You can study for *ifs* qualifications part time while working in a bank or building society. You can also work towards relevant NVQs through assessment in the workplace.

- Most **managers** start as graduate trainees, with a degree in any subject – although subjects related to banking and finance are useful.

- Would-be managers can study for the *ifs* Professional Diploma in Financial Services Management, while in employment. This qualification can allow you to progress on to a degree.

- If you are interested in a career in banking, Diplomas in business, administration and finance are being introduced from 2009.

Find out more

ifs **School of Finance**
IFS House, 4-9 Burgate Lane, Canterbury CT1 2XJ.
Tel: 01227 818609. www.ifslearning.com

The Building Societies Association
6th Floor, York House, 23 Kingsway, London WC2B 6UJ.
Tel: 020 7437 0655. www.bsa.org.uk

Financial Services Skills Council
51 Gresham Street, London EC2V 7HQ.
Tel: 0845 257 3772. www.fssc.org.uk
Contact for general information on Apprenticeships, qualifications etc.

Bar and public house work: see Catering and hospitality

Barrister: see Legal work

Beauty therapy and beauty consultancy

Beauty therapists carry out a wide range of treatments on both the face and the body. They may provide facials, body massage, manicures, pedicures, hair removal treatments, mud wraps, eyelash tinting etc.

Beauty consultants work in shops helping customers to choose cosmetics from the range they sell.

Getting started

- You can train as a **beauty therapist** through a full- or part-time course at your local college. Entry requirements vary, but you may be asked for some GCSEs at grades A*- C, including English, maths and science. Check college prospectuses for details of their courses and entry qualifications.

- Another common entry route for young people is to train in employment through an Apprenticeship or Advanced Apprenticeship in beauty therapy.

- You could also study beauty therapy after A levels or equivalent, through a higher education course. These courses are aimed at potential salon managers.

- As a **beauty consultant**, you would normally be given on-the-job training while working in a department store or for a cosmetics company. Some GCSEs may be required – English, biology and maths are useful subjects. You may be expected to have had some full-time sales experience.

- Beauty consultants have to keep updating their knowledge as products change.

- If you are interested in a career in beauty, Diplomas in hair and beauty studies are being introduced from 2009.

Find out more

Habia

Oxford House, Sixth Avenue, Sky Business Park, Robin Hood Airport, Doncaster DN9 3GG.
Tel: 0845 230 6080. www.habia.org

The Beauty Industry – from the *Real Life Guides* series – published by Trotman, £9.99.

How to Get Ahead in Beauty – published by Heinemann, £12.99.

Bench joinery: see Building crafts

Bilingual secretary: see Language work, Secretarial work

Biochemical engineering: see Engineering

Biochemistry

Biochemists study the structure and function of living things (animals, plants and micro-organisms) at the molecular level. Biochemistry is a practical science that is laboratory-based. It is important to many industries and sectors, including medicine, agriculture, horticulture, veterinary science, forestry, fisheries, brewing and pharmaceuticals.

For a career as a **biochemistry technician**, see *Laboratory technician work*.

Getting started

- You'll need a good base of GCSEs at grades A*-C – including maths, science and an additional science (or biology and chemistry) – to go on to science subjects at A level or equivalent.

- To become a professional biochemist, you need a degree in biochemistry, or in another biological science which includes biochemistry. For entry to a degree course, you are likely to need chemistry A level; other useful subjects are maths, physics and biology.

Find out more

Biochemical Society

Third Floor, Eagle House, 16 Procter Street, London WC1V 6NX. Tel: 020 7280 4100. www.biochemistry.org Careers information is on the website. Publishes the leaflet, *Biochemistry: What, Why and How?*

Careers with a Science Degree – published by Lifetime Publishing, £11.99.

Biology

Modern biologists study plant and animal life at all levels, from molecules to whole ecosystems. They are employed in all sorts of areas, including healthcare, agriculture and horticulture, food technology and academic research.

Getting started

- To become a **biologist**, you need to start by getting good grades at GCSE, or equivalent, in English, maths, science and an additional science (or biology and chemistry).

- For entry to a higher education course in biology, the most suitable AS/A level subjects are biology and chemistry, and either maths, physics or another relevant science. An applied science A level may be acceptable.

- There are also BTEC National courses in applied science offered at colleges of further education. Entry requirements are normally four GCSEs at grades A*-C. A BTEC National qualification can be used for entry to many higher education courses, or to start **technician-level work**.

- At higher-education level, there are courses leading to degrees, HNDs and foundation degrees. You can study 'pure' or 'applied' biology. Applied biology courses look at how biological knowledge can be used, e.g. in agriculture, pollution monitoring and control, or in the food industry.

Find out more

Institute of Biology
9 Red Lion Court, London EC4A 3EF.
Tel: 020 7936 5900. www.iob.org

Careers with a Science Degree – published by Lifetime Publishing, £11.99.

Biomedical science

Biomedical scientists work in hospital pathology and other medical laboratories. They analyse blood, study tissues removed in operations, study bacteria and viruses, and undertake chemical analyses of urine and body fluids.

They are assisted with routine work by **laboratory assistants**, also known as clinical support workers (healthcare science) or healthcare science support workers.

For a career as a biomedical science technician, see *Laboratory technician work.*

Getting started

- To register with the Health Professions Council as a **biomedical scientist**, you need an approved degree and a period of recognised experience.

- For entry to a degree course in biomedical science, you normally need at least two A levels (chemistry and/or biology are usually stipulated), or equivalent, plus supporting GCSEs at grades A*-C.

- While in theory it is possible to gain a trainee post with A levels or equivalent qualifications, and study part time for a degree, employment via this route is now very rare, and normally graduates are recruited.

- There are no formal entry requirements for **laboratory assistants**; sometimes employers ask for a minimum of four GCSEs for more advanced work.

Find out more

Institute of Biomedical Science
12 Coldbath Square, London ECIR 5HL.
Tel: 020 7713 0214. www.ibms.org

NHS Careers
Tel: 0845 60 60 655. www.nhscareers.nhs.uk and
www.stepintothenhs.nhs.uk
Produces a range of careers leaflets.

National Leadership and Innovation Agency for Healthcare
For information on training in Wales, click on 'Careers' on:
www.nliah.wales.nhs.uk

Health Professions Council
Park House, 184 Kennington Park Road, London SE11 4BU.
Tel: 020 7582 0866. www.hpc-uk.org
Website gives details of standards and approved courses.

Careers with a Science Degree – published by Lifetime Publishing,
£11.99.

Working in Hospitals – published by VT Lifeskills, £8.50. Includes a profile
of a medical laboratory assistant.

Botany: see Biology

Brewing technology

Technical brewers supervise the beer brewing process and have to be
able to work out how to solve any problems. They need to understand
the engineering and biochemical processes and have to know all about
ingredients and recipes. In a large brewery, a brewer may specialise in
one or two areas, such as fermentation or packaging. In a small brewery,
they are likely to be in charge of all stages of production. **Brewing
scientists** work in quality control or in research and development,
creating new beers. They advise brewery managers on the technical
aspects of beer production. They analyse both the ingredients and the
finished products.

Getting started

- Brewing scientists and technical brewers are mainly graduates
  of chemistry, microbiology or biochemistry (or applied

branches of these subjects). You'll need A levels in science or mathematical subjects (or equivalent qualifications) to get on a degree course, plus supporting GCSEs. Some scientists have postgraduate qualifications too.

- Brewers normally sit the examinations of the Institute of Brewing and Distilling.

- You could also work in a brewery as an engineer, dealing with equipment, processes and systems. See *Engineering* for details of how to qualify.

Find out more

Institute of Brewing and Distilling
33 Clarges Street, London W1J 7EE.
Tel: 020 7499 8144. www.ibd.org.uk
Produces the guide – *A General Guide to Technical Careers in the Brewing Industry.*

Working in Science – published by VT Lifeskills, £8.50. Includes a profile of a brewer.

Bricklaying: see Building crafts

Broadcasting: see Media: radio, TV, film and video/DVD

Building crafts

The construction industry employs more than 10% of the British workforce producing new buildings and new roads, bridges, tunnels and railways as well as repairing and renovating those that we already have. There is a wide range of skilled craft-level careers suitable for people who like working with their hands. For higher-level careers, see *Building technician and technologist work.*

These are just some of the jobs for craftsmen and women in the construction industry.

Bench joiners make parts of buildings, such as doors, windows, staircases and fitted furniture out of wood. They are usually based in a workshop inside and rarely work on a construction site.

Bricklayers work on construction sites building walls with bricks and blocks using a trowel and mortar.

Carpenters and joiners work with wood, making and fitting doors, window frames, staircases and floorboards. Many items are made in a factory and fitted on site.

Demolition workers use equipment and explosives to demolish unwanted buildings safely.

Electricians install the wiring and electrical systems in new buildings, and rewire old ones. They need normal colour vision to identify different coloured wires.

Glaziers cut glass and other window materials to size and fit them in place.

Painters and decorators paint inside and outside a building and put up wallpaper.

Plant operators drive the heavy machinery on a construction site operating the earth-moving equipment and the cranes.

Plasterers prepare and apply plaster to inside walls and ceilings. They also make ornamental plasterwork in workshops away from construction sites.

Plumbers put water, heating and gas systems in new buildings, as well as repairing them in existing buildings.

Roof tilers and slaters fix tiles and slates to roofs after covering the rafters with roofing felt.

Scaffolders put up scaffolding allowing access to all parts of the building.

Steeplejacks carry out a wide range of repair work on very high buildings like church spires and industrial chimneys.

Stonemasons shape, prepare and fix stone blocks, working in workshops and on site.

Wall and floor tilers fix tiles to the floors and walls in bathrooms, kitchens and in large areas like swimming pools.

In many small building firms, craftsmen and women undertake a number of different crafts.

Getting started

- You may need GCSEs at grade E or above in English, maths, science and technology for trainee vacancies. Training schemes include Apprenticeships and Advanced Apprenticeships and the Construction Apprenticeship Scheme. Training takes place in a college or training centre as well as at the workplace with trainees working towards NVQs.

- There are also full-time college courses in construction crafts.

- Some 14- to 16-year-olds may have the opportunity to take a Young Apprenticeship in construction, combining learning and work experience with an employer with study at school and college.

- If you are interested in a career in building, Diplomas in construction and the built environment may be available.

Find out more

ConstructionSkills
Tel: 01485 577577 (for details of your local office).
www.bconstructive.co.uk

Working in the Built Environment & Construction – published by VT Lifeskills, £8.50.

Construction, Carpentry and Cabinet-Making, Electrician and *Plumbing* – four titles from the *Real Life Guides* series – published by Trotman, £9.99 each.

How to Get Ahead in Construction – published by Heinemann, £12.99.

Building services engineering

Building services engineers make our living and working environments more pleasant and convenient. They provide our buildings with essential services such as light, heat, air conditioning, ventilation and refrigeration. They may also deal with acoustics, communications, power and water supply, and they make sure energy is used efficiently and safely. Professional **engineers** plan the systems, and **technicians** and **craftsmen and women** install and maintain them.

Getting started

- You can start training for craft- or technician-level work with good GCSEs in maths, English and science, or equivalent.

- Apprenticeships and Advanced Apprenticeships are available for young people. There are also full- and part-time college courses.

- To be a professional engineer, you need a degree, plus further study and training. For details of the different training routes and levels of work, see *Engineering*.

- If you are interested in building services engineering, Diplomas in engineering may be available.

Find out more

Building Engineering Services Training Ltd
The Mere, Second Floor, Milestone House, Upton Park, Slough, Berkshire SL1 2DQ.
Tel: 01753 531188. www.best-ltd.co.uk

Working in the Built Environment & Construction – published by VT Lifeskills, £8.50.

Construction – from the *Real Life Guides* series – published by Trotman, £9.99.

Building surveying: see Surveying

Building technician and technologist work

Building technicians and technologists work on construction sites and in the offices of construction companies. Taking the designs produced by architects and civil engineers, the building professionals estimate the costs, purchase the materials and plan the schedule for completion. They supervise the building work, making sure that deadlines are kept to and that standards are maintained. They need to be able to communicate well with both clients and builders. Seeing a building project through to its completion can be very satisfying.

Getting started

- Your first step is to get GCSEs at grades A*-C in maths, sciences and English, as you need at least A level or a BTEC National qualification in construction to work as a technician.

- It's possible to gain qualifications by part-time study while working as a building craftsman or woman, or to work your way up through NVQs.

- Advanced Apprenticeships are one entry route for young people, leading to NVQ level 3.

- There are full-time, part-time and sandwich courses leading to foundation degrees, HNDs and degrees in subjects like building studies, construction management and building technology.

- For entry to a degree course, you need to specialise in maths and physical sciences - or possibly construction and the built environment - at A level or equivalent.

- If you are interested in building work, Diplomas in construction and the built environment may be available.

Find out more

ConstructionSkills
Tel: 01485 577577 (for details of your local office).
www.bconstructive.co.uk

Working in the Built Environment & Construction - published by VT Lifeskills, £8.50.

Construction - from the *Real Life Guides* series - published by Trotman, £9.99.

Business management: see Management

Buying: see Purchasing and stock control, Retailing

Cardiac technician work: see Medical technology

Care assistance: see Social work

Careers work

Personal advisers or careers advisers give guidance to young people and adults on their choice of career, training opportunities and further and higher education. Most of them work for Connexions or careers services, and interview clients at the Connexions/careers centre or in schools, colleges and youth centres. Some group work is involved, and there's lots of computerised record keeping! Some work for private careers guidance agencies, or in universities. Within the Connexions service, personal advisers offer guidance on many other topics which affect young people, besides careers.

Getting started

- This isn't a job you go into straight from school. Training is for graduates, or for adults with appropriate skills and experience.

- One-year, full-time or two-year, part-time training courses (which include work-based training with an employer) lead to the Qualification in Careers Guidance (QCG).

- To work in Connexions or careers services, you also need an NVQ level 4 in advice and guidance work.

- There is an additional Diploma for Connexions Personal Advisers, gained through in-service training.

- If you are already working in a Connexions or careers service, you can gain NVQs in the workplace.

Find out more

Institute of Career Guidance
Third Floor, Copthall House, 1 New Road Stourbridge, West Midlands DY8 1PH.
Tel: 01384 376464. www.icg-uk.org

Working in Advice & Counselling – published by VT Lifeskills, £8.50. Includes a profile of a careers adviser.

Carpentry: see Building crafts

Cartography

Cartographers make maps from information provided by land surveyors, from aerial photographs and satellite imagery. There are jobs with the Ordnance Survey, other government departments such as the Ministry of Defence, the Forestry Commission, the Met Office or with local authorities. There are also posts with commercial map publishers and the exploration departments of oil companies. Much of the work is computerised. There are not many jobs, so entry is very competitive.

Getting started

- There are a very few opportunities to start as a trainee after A levels in geography and maths, or equivalent.

- You can study for a degree in cartography, mapping sciences or geographic information systems, or for a geography degree which includes cartography. Entry requirements are two or more A levels, plus a good base of GCSEs at grades A*-C. Useful subjects include maths, geography, science, ICT and a foreign language. Relevant vocational qualifications, such as BTEC National in construction which cover surveying, may be acceptable for entry to some courses.

- You can also gain a postgraduate qualification in cartography, after a degree in geography or another relevant subject.

Find out more

British Cartographic Society
c/o Royal Geographical Society, Kensington Gore, London SW7 2AR.
Tel: 01823 665775. www.cartography.org.uk

Catering and hospitality

The hospitality and catering industry covers the jobs that provide food, drink, accommodation and other services in a wide variety of settings. Food may be provided by restaurants, pubs, takeaways, college canteens and hospitals, while accommodation ranges from luxury hotels to small guesthouses and college halls of residence. There are jobs at all levels, including **kitchen assistants, hotel receptionists, bar staff, waiters/ waitresses, housekeepers, chefs** and **managers**. A manager may be in charge of a single restaurant or pub, or a whole chain of hotels.

Getting started

- You can start in a job in hotel reception, cookery or domestic work and, by taking NVQs from levels 1-5, progress to supervisory and management grades.

- You can gain work-related qualifications in hospitality and catering at some schools and colleges. It's possible to work your way up through BTEC National qualifications or similar, to Higher National qualifications and degrees. Or you can progress from almost any A level subjects to higher education courses in catering and hospitality management.

- Young people can enter the industry through Apprenticeships and Advanced Apprenticeships, leading to NVQs at levels 2 and 3 respectively.

- Once you are working in the industry, with two years' supervisory experience, you can study part-time for the qualifications offered by the Institute of Hospitality.

- Some 14- to 16-year-olds may have the opportunity to take a Young Apprenticeship in hospitality combining learning and work experience with an employer with study at school and college.

- If you are interested in a career in catering and hospitality, Diplomas in hospitality are being introduced from 2009.

Find out more

British Hospitality Association
Queens House, 55-56 Lincoln's Inn Fields, London WC2A 3BH.
Tel: 020 7404 7744. www.bha.org.uk

People 1st
2nd Floor, Armstrong House, 38 Market Square, Uxbridge UB8 1LH.
Tel: 0870 060 2550. www.people1st.co.uk and www.springboarduk.org

Working in Food & Drink and *Working in Hospitality & Catering* – both published by VT Lifeskills, £8.50 each.

Catering – from the *Real Life Guides* series – published by Trotman, £9.99.

How to Get Ahead in Catering – published by Heinemann, £12.99.

Ceramics: see Art and design

Chemical engineering: see Engineering

Chemistry

Chemistry is all about understanding what different substances are made of, and how this knowledge can be used. **Chemists** work in the community, health services and education. In industry, they may work in research and development, production or quality control. They are involved in the manufacture of detergents, plastics, food products, packaging, man-made fibres, medicines, petrol, paints and dyestuffs – and many more everyday things which we take for granted.

Chemists are graduates, but there are also opportunities at **technician** or **laboratory assistant** level, for people with fewer qualifications. Warning: the person who works in a chemist's shop preparing drugs is a pharmacist and not a chemist!

Getting started

- To work in chemistry at any level, you need to get GCSE science and an additional science (or two separate sciences, if your school offers them) at grades A*-C.

- For entry to technician-level work, or to get onto a degree course, you will also need chemistry at A level (plus another science or maths), an applied science A level, or a BTEC National qualification in science. You should check exact requirements for courses which interest you.

- Trainee technicians usually study part time for BTEC National qualifications, perhaps followed by an HNC or foundation degree.

- You can specialise in different areas of chemistry on either HND or degree courses.

- Entry onto an HND course usually requires one science A level or equivalent.

- Research scientists usually have a postgraduate qualification.

- Advanced Apprenticeships offer young people a route into the chemical industry, leading to NVQ level 3.

- Some 14- to 16-year-olds may have the opportunity to take a Young Apprenticeship in science, combining learning and work experience with an employer with study at school and college.

Find out more

The Royal Society of Chemistry

The Education Department, Burlington House, Piccadilly, London W1J 0BA.

Tel: 020 7440 3344. www.rsc.org/Education/SchoolStudents and www.chemsoc.org

Careers with a Science Degree – published by Lifetime Publishing, £11.99.

Working in Science – published by VT Lifeskills, £8.50. Includes a profile of a chemistry research associate.

Children – work with: see Early years childcare and education, Nursing, Social work, Teaching

---

Chiropody: see Podiatry

Chiropractic and osteopathy

Chiropractors and **osteopaths** help people with back pain and other problems, mostly by using their hands to manipulate the spine and joints. Increasingly, they are able to work within, or in association with, the NHS, although most work from private clinics. They are graduates of their particular specialism, and have to be registered. Some osteopaths and chiropractors choose to specialise in work with animals.

Getting started

- To be a **chiropractor**, you need a degree approved by the General Chiropractic Council. To be an **osteopath**, your degree must be approved by the General Osteopathic Council.

- For either degree, you need at least two A levels, including sciences, or an equivalent qualification. You must first get a range of supporting GCSEs, including sciences, at grades A*-C.

- Degree courses may be full or part time.

- Alternatively, you can qualify through an approved postgraduate course, after gaining a relevant first degree.

Find out more

The General Osteopathic Council
Osteopathy House, 176 Tower Bridge Road, London SE1 3LU.
Tel: 020 7357 6655. www.osteopathy.org.uk

General Chiropractic Council
44 Wicklow Street, London WC1X 9HL.
Tel: 020 7713 5155. www.gcc-uk.org

Civil engineering: see Engineering

Civil Service

There are hundreds of different jobs which come under the banner of the Civil Service. Some civil servants work directly for government ministers, researching and advising on the formulation of policy. The majority work in head or local offices or executive agencies applying this policy, whether it's paying out benefits, dealing with regional transport strategies or managing prisons. Many jobs involve dealing with the public.

Over 170 different departments and agencies employ civil servants. These range from huge departments like the Department for Children, Schools and Families and the Home Office, to smaller concerns such as the Intellectual Property Office and the Veterinary Laboratories Agency. 80% of civil servants work outside London. As well as administrative posts, there are professional, scientific and technical posts in the Civil Service, such as those held by librarians, cartographers and meteorologists. These are dealt with under the relevant headings elsewhere in this Careers Guide. Specialist posts include those in HM Revenue and Customs, the UK Border Agency and the Diplomatic Service.

Getting started

- Departments carry out their own recruitment locally, and set their own entry requirements – except for graduate Fast Stream entrants who are recruited centrally.

- You can start at a junior level straight from school, with good GCSEs (including English) or A levels or equivalent.

- There are opportunities for promotion to junior management grades; most new entrants at junior manager level are graduates.

- There are jobs for graduates of many subjects, including economics, law, engineering, science and languages. Many departments have their own graduate training schemes.

- To apply to join the general Fast Stream Development Programme, which prepares people for the very top jobs, you'll need a good base of GCSEs at grades A*-C , followed by A levels or equivalent and a first- or second-class honours degree.

- There are specialist Fast Streams for science and engineering graduates and for would-be diplomats.

Find out more

For information on careers and recruitment, and a job-search facility, visit the **Civil Service Recruitment Gateway** website: www.careers.civil-service.gov.uk

Civil Service Fast Stream
Pilgrims Well, 427 London Road, Camberley, Surrey GU15 3HZ.
Tel: 01276 400333. www.faststream.gov.uk

Clerical work: see Civil Service, Local government administration, Secretarial work

---

Communications engineering: see Engineering

Community justice work: see Probation work and community justice

Community nursing: see Nursing

Community work: see Probation work and community justice, Youth and community work

Company secretarial work

A company secretary is a highly-qualified administrator, who acts as a company's legal representative and ensures that it operates within the law. Company secretaries are responsible for keeping a register of shareholders and calling shareholders' meetings, paying dividends on shares and organising Board meetings. They may also advise the Board on financial and legal matters. In some companies the company secretary may also carry out personnel and other administrative functions.

Getting started

- You can study for the examinations of the Institute of Chartered Secretaries and Administrators (ICSA) on a full-time college course, on a part-time course while you are working, or by distance learning.

- There are three parts to the qualification: the ICSA Certificate in Business Practice, the ICSA Diploma in Business Practice and the ICSA Professional Programme.

- You can study for the ICSA Certificate in Business Practice without formal academic qualifications.

- The Institute's examinations are also useful if you want to enter other areas of administrative work.

Find out more

Institute of Chartered Secretaries and Administrators (ICSA)
16 Park Crescent, London W1B 1AH.
Tel: 020 7580 4741. www.icsa.org.uk

Complementary medicine

Many people now seek help from therapists and practitioners of complementary medicine, instead of – or as well as – seeing their usual doctor. Some of these therapies started in ancient times and in different cultures.

Most areas of complementary medicine have some sort of registration scheme and code of practice. There is likely to be statutory regulation of certain treatments, such as acupuncture and herbal medicine, in the future. The Institute for Complementary Medicine maintains the British Register of Complementary Practitioners, and can provide information on training for a wide range of disciplines. The Complementary and Natural Healthcare Council is being launched to provide a regulatory structure; registration will be voluntary.

Getting started

- Training routes vary from short courses to degree-level or even postgraduate qualifications.

- If you already know which area of complementary medicine you are interested in, contact the appropriate organisation given below. There are many other organisations which we do not have room to list here.

- There may be more than one training route and professional body for an area of work.

- To set yourself up in private practice, you will need to develop your communication skills so that you can relate well to clients, and look into the legal and financial side of self-employment.

Find out more

Complementary and Natural Healthcare Council
www.fih.org.uk

Institute for Complementary Medicine
Unit 25, Tavern Quay Business Centre, Sweden Gate London SE16 7TX.
Tel: 020 7231 5855. www.i-c-m.co.uk

British Acupuncture Council
63 Jeddo Road, London W12 9HQ.
Tel: 020 8735 0400. www.acupuncture.org.uk

Society of Teachers of the Alexander Technique
1st Floor, Linton House, 39-51 Highgate Road, London NW5 1RS.
Tel: 0845 230 7828. www.stat.org.uk

International Federation of Aromatherapists
61-63 Churchfield Road, Acton, London W3 6AY.
Tel: 020 8992 9605. www.ifaroma.org

National Institute of Medical Herbalists
Elm House, 54 Mary Arches Street, Exeter EX4 3BA.
Tel: 01392 426022. www.nimh.org.uk

The Society of Homoeopaths
11 Brookfield, Duncan Close, Moulton Park, Northampton NN3 6WL.
Tel: 0845 450 6611. www.homeopathy-soh.org

Incorporated Society of Registered Naturopaths
328 Harrogate Road, Leeds LS17 6PE.
Tel: 0113 268 5992. www.registerednaturopaths.org

Association of Reflexologists
5 Fore Street, Taunton, Somerset TA1 1HX.
Tel: 0870 567 3320. www.aor.org.uk

The Shiatsu Society of the UK
PO Box 4580, Rugby CV21 9EL.
LTel: 0845 130 4560. www.shiatsu.org

Computer engineering: see Information and communication technology

---

Computer-aided design: see Art and design

Computing: see Information and communication technology

Conservation work (arts): see Museum work

Construction work: see Building crafts

Consumer advice work: see Trading standards

Crafts: see Art and design

Creative therapies

Creative therapists use art, drama, music, dance, play and horticulture to help people with psychiatric or emotional problems to express themselves. It is very demanding work, and posts (usually part-time) are scarce. Therapists may work in hospitals, clinics, special schools and prisons. This is normally a career move for adults already experienced in their art form, or in teaching, healthcare, occupational therapy etc.

Getting started

- You usually need a degree in your subject, followed by postgraduate training, to be an **art**, **drama** or **music therapist**. Alternatively, a degree or equivalent qualification in another subject or profession, plus proven ability in the therapy subject, can lead to postgraduate training.

- Art, drama and music therapists have to be registered by the Health Professions Council.

- **Dance movement therapy** is not as structured a profession as art, drama and music therapy, but the Association for Dance Movement Therapy UK administers its own register of therapists. There are a few postgraduate courses and distance learning programmes are available to dance teachers, social workers or others interested in community therapeutic dance.

- If you have already gained experience working with children, you can take an intensive training course in **play therapy**, validated by the British Association of Play Therapists.

- Thrive runs Diploma and Certificate courses in **therapeutic horticulture**, as well as short courses. The Diploma is open to graduates in horticulture or a caring profession, as well as to holders of the Certificate.

Find out more

Health Professions Council
Park House, 184 Kennington Park Road, London SE11 4BU.
Tel: 020 7582 0866. www.hpc-uk.org
Website gives details of standards and approved courses.

Association for Dance Movement Therapy UK
32 Meadowfoot Lane, Torquay TQ1 2BW.
www.admt.org.uk

Thrive
The Geoffrey Udall Centre, Beech Hill, Reading RG7 2AT.
Tel: 0118 988 5688. www.thrive.org.uk
Careers in therapeutic horticulture can be viewed on the website

British Association of Play Therapists
1 Beacon Mews, South Road, Weybridge, Surrey KT13 9DZ.
Tel: 01932 828638. www.bapt.uk.com
Website offers case studies of play therapists plus publications to order.

Working in Community Healthcare – published by VT Lifeskills, £8.50.
Includes profiles of an art therapist and a music therapist.

Curator: see Museum work

Customer services

The customer may not always be right, but good customer service is important in any organisation that provides goods or services to the public. If a complaint or query is poorly handled, that customer may never come back – and may give the organisation a bad reputation. Some of the work is face-to-face, particularly in retail organisations, but most is by telephone – perhaps in a call centre or customer contact centre. Employers include financial services, tour operators, the telecommunications industry, manufacturing firms, utilities and many more!

Getting started

- You need the right personality for a start, with good communication skills and a patient and polite manner. And you need to stay calm under pressure.

- You can train straight from school, through a company in-house training programme. Some good grades at GCSE, including maths and English, may be required.

- There are Apprenticeships and Advanced Apprenticeships in call handling and in customer service for young people, leading to NVQ levels 2 and 3 respectively.

- You'll need to learn all about your employer's goods or services – and that may include technical information.

- College courses in business, retail and distribution, marketing or public relations can be useful.

- You can work towards membership of the Institute of Customer Service, through their own qualifications or through NVQs.

Find out more

Institute of Customer Service
2 Castle Court, St Peter's Street, Colchester CO1 1EW.
Tel: 01206 571716. www.instituteofcustomerservice.com

Working in Retail & Customer Services – published by VT Lifeskills, £8.50.

Cybernetics: see Engineering

Dairy farming: see Farming and agricultural advisory work

Dance movement therapy: see Creative therapies

Dancing

Dancers may work as stage performers of ballet and contemporary and modern dance, teach children and adults, plan dance sequences (which is known as choreography) or work in administration and management. To be a performer you need to be dedicated, as well as talented.

Getting started

- To be a **performer**, there are no set entry requirements. You need to be very talented, dedicated and self-disciplined. You can apply for funded places directly to independent dance and drama colleges, and selection is through an audition. Courses normally lead to a degree, diploma or certificate. CDET accredits professional dance training courses.

- There are some degree courses – dance studies, community dance etc – which are not performance-based. For these, you need some practical dance experience, as well as the usual academic qualifications. For the courses leading to **Qualified Teacher Status** (to teach in schools), the entrance requirements are the same as those of other teaching courses.

- Some 14- to 16-year-olds may have the opportunity to take a Young Apprenticeship in performing arts, combining learning and work experience with an employer with study at school and college.

- GCSEs, AS/A levels and other qualifications are available in performing arts.

Find out more

Council for Dance Education and Training (CDET)
Old Brewer's Yard, 17-19 Neal Street, Covent Garden, London WC2H 9UY.
Tel: 020 7240 5703. www.cdet.org.uk
A range of information leaflets covering various areas of dance training is available on their website.

The Arts Council England
Dance Department, 14 Great Peter Street, London SW1P 3NQ.
Tel: 0845 300 6200. www.artscouncil.org.uk

Working in Performing Arts – published by VT Lifeskills, £8.50.

Performing Arts Uncovered – published by Trotman, £11.99.

Database management: see Information and communication technology

---

Decorating: see Building crafts

Demolition work: see Building crafts

Dental hygiene work

Dental hygienists carry out treatments prescribed by dentists. They scale, clean and polish teeth, check for signs of gum disease, apply preventive materials that help reduce dental decay, and teach people how to look after their teeth.

Getting started

- Training is normally through a 27-month, full-time diploma course. Three-year degree courses are also available.

- To start the diploma course, you need at least two A levels, or the equivalent, plus supporting GCSEs at grades A*-C, including English and a science, preferably biology, or a nationally-recognised qualification such as the National Certificate in dental nursing.

Find out more

British Society of Dental Hygiene and Therapy
3 Kestrel Court, Waterwells Business Park, Waterwells Drive, Quedgeley, Gloucester GL2 2AT.
Tel: 0870 243 0752. www.bsdht.org.uk
The website includes lists of training schools.

Dental nursing

Dental nurses help the dentist by preparing materials and equipment, assisting at the chairside, sterilising instruments, looking after patients and doing paperwork. Dental nurses need to be gentle and sympathetic with patients who are often nervous or distressed.

Getting started

- You can do a part-time day release or evening course while working in general practice, to gain the National Certificate in dental nursing. There are no academic entry requirements. The exam can be taken at any time, but the Certificate is not awarded until you also have at least two years' chairside experience. Some courses lead to NVQs at levels 2 and 3 in oral healthcare.

- Full-time courses at schools of dental nursing at dental teaching hospitals lead to the National Certificate/NVQs. You may need some GCSEs at grades A*-C, depending on the hospital.

- There are a few full-time courses at further education colleges which lead to the National Certificate. There may be special entry requirements.

Find out more

British Association of Dental Nurses

PO Box 4, Room 200, Hill House International Business Centre, Thornton-Cleveleys FY5 4QD.
Tel: 01253 338360. www.badn.org.uk

National Examining Board for Dental Nurses

110 London Street, Fleetwood, Lancashire FY7 6EU.
Tel: 01253 778417. www.nebdn.org

Working in Community Healthcare – published by VT Lifeskills, £8.50. Includes a profile of a dental nurse.

Dental technician work

Dental technicians construct and repair false teeth, bridges, crowns and the orthodontic appliances which are used for straightening teeth. They work to a prescription from a dentist.

Getting started

- You can train for four to five years, combining part-time study with on-the-job training in a laboratory, for the BTEC National Diploma in dental technology. You need four GCSEs at grades A*-C to start; maths and science may be required subjects, although this can vary.

- Four-year hospital training schemes, which include some college study, are offered by some hospitals or health authorities.

- There are three-year, full-time courses at some colleges of further education, leading to the BTEC Diploma. There are also a couple of degree courses in dental technology, for which you need at least two A levels or the equivalent, plus supporting GCSEs as mentioned above.

Find out more

Dental Technologists Association
Waterwells Drive, Waterwells Business Park, Gloucester GL2 2AT.
Tel: 0870 243 0753. www.dta-uk.org

The Dental Laboratories Association Ltd
44-46 Wollaton Road, Beeston, Nottinghamshire NG9 2NR.
Tel: 0115 925 4888. www.dla.org.uk
The Dental Technology Student's Prospectus can be downloaded.

Dental therapy work

Dental therapists work under the direction of a dentist in a dental practice, a hospital, community dental service or school dental clinic. They do simple fillings, extract milk teeth and scale and polish teeth.

Getting started

- There is a 27-month, full-time course leading to the Diploma in Dental Therapy, which also includes qualification as a dental hygienist. Three-year degree courses are also available.

- For entry to the Diploma course, you need two A levels, or the equivalent, plus five GCSEs at grades A*-C to start. If you don't have A levels, a nationally-recognised Dental Nursing Certificate may be an acceptable alternative.

Find out more

The British Dental Association
64 Wimpole Street, London W1G 8YS.
Tel: 020 7935 0875. www.bda.org.uk

British Association of Dental Therapists
www.badt.org.uk

Dentistry

Dentists conserve teeth by filling, crowning and bridgework and try to prevent dental disease. They take out teeth and design false teeth to replace them. They correct irregular teeth in children by using plates and braces: this is called **orthodontics**. Dentists need to be aware that some people find visits to the dentist frightening. They must also be skilled with their hands.

Getting started

- A five-year degree in dentistry is essential.

- For entry to a degree course you normally need three A levels at very good grades, plus supporting GCSEs at grades A*-C. Most schools of dentistry require chemistry and/or biology A level (at least at AS level if not A level).

Find out more

The British Dental Association
64 Wimpole Street, London W1G 8YS.
Tel: 020 7935 0875. www.bda.org.uk

Working in Community Healthcare – published by VT Lifeskills, £8.50. Includes a profile of a dentist.

Design: see Art and design

Dietetics

Dietitians are trained specialists who apply the science of nutrition to everyday eating by promoting good food habits in people of all ages. Many work in hospitals where they teach and advise patients on diet for certain diseases; others work in the community advising groups of people, particularly older people and children, on healthy eating.

Getting started

- There are four-year degree courses in dietetics and nutrition. For entry to a degree course, you need at least two A levels or the equivalent, plus supporting GCSEs at grades A*-C. A level subjects should normally include chemistry and another science.

- Dietitians must be registered with the Health Professions Council.

Find out more

The British Dietetic Association
5th Floor, Charles House, 148/149 Great Charles Street, Queensway, Birmingham B3 3HT.
Tel: 0121 200 8080. www.bda.uk.com

Health Professions Council
Park House, 184 Kennington Road, London SE11 4BU.
Tel: 020 7582 0866. www.hpc-uk.org
Website gives details of standards and approved courses.

Working in Community Healthcare – published by VT Lifeskills, £8.50.
Includes a profile of a dietitian.

Dispensing optics

Dispensing opticians supply and fit glasses and contact lenses prescribed by a specially qualified doctor or an optometrist (ophthalmic optician). They do not test eyesight.

Getting started

- There are part-time courses at colleges of further education and correspondence courses, working towards the examinations of the Association of British Dispensing Opticians (ABDO). Qualification takes three years.

- There are a couple of two-year, full-time courses for the examination of the ABDO. You would also need a year's practical experience following the final examination.

- You need at least five GCSEs at grades A*-C, including English, maths and science for both the above qualification routes.

- Alternatively, you could follow a full-time degree course in ophthalmic dispensing.

Find out more

Association of British Dispensing Opticians (ABDO) College
Godmersham Park Mansion, Godmersham, Canterbury CT4 7DT.
Tel: 01227 738829. www.abdo.org.uk

Display work: see Art and design

Distribution: see Logistics and transport

District nursing: see Nursing

Doctor: see Medicine and surgery

Drama

Apart from acting, there are careers in **stage production**, **stage management** and **teaching**. **Actors** can spend periods of time without work, so you will need to think about alternative ways of earning money during 'quiet' periods.

Getting started

- There are three-year, full-time courses in acting or stage management at drama schools. Academic qualifications are not as important as evidence of your acting potential, although many drama students have GCSEs and A levels. There are scholarships for some students attending accredited courses. Selection depends on an audition. Competition is fierce.

- There are degree courses in acting, in drama and related subjects, and a recognised course for teachers. Some courses are academic and are not stage training – so check course content carefully. Some accredited degree courses attract scholarships.

- Some 14- to 16-year-olds may have the opportunity to take a Young Apprenticeship in performing arts, combining work experience with an employer with study at school and college.

- GCSE, AS/A level and other qualifications are available in performing arts.

Find out more

National Council for Drama Training
1-7 Woburn Walk, London WCIH OJJ.
Tel: 020 7387 3650. www.ncdt.co.uk
Can provide information about drama schools and accredited courses.

Working in Performing Arts – published by VT Lifeskills, £8.50.

Performing Arts Uncovered – published by Trotman, £11.99.

Dramatherapy: see Creative therapies

Driving instructing and examining

Driving instructors mainly work on a one-to-one basis giving people tuition in specially adapted cars. Some driving instructors teach people how to drive buses and large goods vehicles. Instructors need patience, and the ability to keep a cool head. **Driving examiners** test learner drivers.

Getting started

- To become a **driving instructor**, you must pass the written and practical tests of the Driving Standards Agency (DSA), and be registered. You must be at least 21 before you can apply to take the tests. There are no specific educational qualifications.

- **Driving examiners** must have held a full driving licence continuously for the last four years and have no more than three penalty points. They must also pass an exam, driving test and interview, before training to be an examiner for the DSA.

Find out more

Driving Instructors Association (DSA)
Safety House, Beddington Farm Road, Croydon CR0 4XZ.
Tel: 020 8665 5151. www.driving.org

Working in Transport & Logistics – published by VT Lifeskills, £8.50. Includes a profile of a driving instructor.

Driving lorries/trucks: see Logistics and transport

Early years childcare and education

Early years staff work in nurseries and pre-schools with children under school age, as nannies in private households and in crèches attached to leisure centres and colleges. They also work in primary schools and other settings, with children up to eight years. Some experienced staff set up their own businesses running private nurseries or childminding in their own homes.

Getting started

- **Nannies** working in private households don't have to be qualified or registered, although most employers look for a recognised childcare qualification.

- **Childminders** do not have to hold formal qualifications but must be Ofsted-registered, and meet certain requirements.

- There are full- and part-time college courses leading to qualifications offered by CACHE, such as the level 2 Certificate, and the level 3 Diploma in Child Care and Education. For entry to the level 3 Diploma, most colleges require a number of GCSEs at grades A*-C or equivalent (such as the level 2 Certificate).

- NVQs in children's care, learning and development are available, which can be gained by assessment within the workplace, and through attendance at a part-time course whilst in employment.

- There are a number of private nursery colleges offering CACHE qualifications and their own awards. The better known private colleges usually ask for at least five GCSEs at grades A*-C, including English, for entry to the CACHE level 3 Diploma.

- You may be able to train through an Apprenticeship or Advanced Apprenticeship.

Find out more

CACHE (Council for Awards in Children's Care and Education)
Beaufort House, Grosvenor Road, St Albans, Hertfordshire AL1 3AW.
Tel: 0845 347 2123. www.cache.org.uk
For information about qualifications.

Professional Association of Nursery Nurses
2 St James's Court, Friar Gate, Derby DE1 1BT.
Tel: 01332 372337. www.pat.org.uk
Produces the information pack, *All You Need to Know about Working as a Nanny*.

More information about working with young children can be found on: www.childcarecareers.gov.uk

Economics

Economists advise businesses and the Government on economic issues which affect future plans and decision-making, by looking at resources – money, raw materials, goods, services and people – and advising on their best use.

Getting started

- You have to hold a degree in economics. For entry, you need at least two A levels, or the equivalent, plus GCSEs at grades A*-C including maths. A level maths is always useful.

- GCSE and AS/A levels in economics are available. Although these are rarely needed for degree course entry, studying the subject will give you an idea of whether you would enjoy it at a higher level.

Find out more

Government Economic Service
Economics in Government, HM Treasury, 1 Horse Guards Road, London W1A 2HQ.
Tel: 020 7270 4571/5073. www.ges.gov.uk

Editing: see Publishing

Electrical engineering: see Engineering

Electrician work: see Building crafts

Electronic engineering: see Engineering

Embalming: see Funeral work

Energy engineering: see Engineering

Engineering

Engineering covers an extremely wide field of careers. This section deals with the work of chartered engineers, incorporated engineers and engineering technicians. Engineers need to be creative, good at solving problems and being part of a team.

- **Aeronautical engineers** design airframes and the systems (such as heating and ventilation) within the aircraft. They also service and repair aircraft for airline operators.

- **Chemical and biochemical engineers** study industrial processes and design, construct and operate the plant in which they take place. Safety and environmental issues are very important.

- **Civil engineers** plan, design, construct and maintain roads, railways, airports, bridges, tunnels, water supplies and reservoirs, and the supply and distribution of energy.

- **Electrical engineers** are responsible for generating electricity, to provide a continuous source of power for equipment used in homes, schools, offices and hospitals.

- **Electronics engineers** work in communications, developing highly sophisticated computers and information systems, for use in telecommunications, transport, business, industry and medicine. Some engineers specialise in robotics, cybernetics and mechatronics.

- **Energy engineers** are responsible for the preparation and burning of coal, gas, oil and nuclear fuel for heating, lighting and power. Gas engineering covers both civil engineering – the provision of pipelines and gas holders – and chemical engineering, producing gas from coal or oil and the exploration for further gas supplies.

- **Marine engineers** design, construct, operate and maintain ships' engines and systems. Many work in the Royal Navy and Merchant Navy as engineer officers; others work in offshore and ocean engineering.

- **Mechanical engineers** design, manufacture, install, operate and maintain machinery of all kinds. They work in fields as diverse as biomechanics, satellite systems, nuclear power, materials science and food technologies.

- **Mining and minerals engineers** design and manage mining operations so they are profitable, safe and harm the environment as little as possible.

- **Naval architects** are concerned with the design, construction, repair, maintenance and surveying of ships, boats and offshore structures.

Getting started

- Some 14- to 16-year-olds may have the opportunity to take a Young Apprenticeship in engineering, combining learning and work experience with an employer with study at school and college.

- GCSEs, AS/A levels and Diplomas in engineering are available in some schools and colleges, but check the acceptability of these courses if you wish to enter training to become a professional engineer.

Chartered engineer (CEng)

- You need to follow an accredited MEng degree course, followed by a period of professional development in work, and a final review. To enter a degree course, you need three very good A levels, including maths and physics, or the equivalent, plus supporting GCSEs at grades A*-C. Equivalent qualifications may be accepted. People with a BEng degree can do further study and training to become a chartered engineer.

Incorporated engineer (IEng)

- You need to follow an accredited BEng degree course, followed by a period of professional development in work, and a final review. To enter a degree course, you need A levels in maths and physics or another science subject, plus supporting GCSEs at grades A*-C.

- There are HNC/HND and foundation degree courses accredited by the Engineering Council, for which you normally need one or two A levels or the equivalent. You can follow a further period of study and training to reach degree-level standard.

- Alternative routes to get you started include foundation courses for those without the correct A levels, Higher Apprenticeships and Engineering Council exams.

Engineering Technician (EngTech)

- Most training is through an Advanced Apprenticeship. Employers usually ask for a minimum of four GCSEs at grades A*-C to include maths, science and English, or the equivalent. To reach EngTech status requires a period of work to develop your skills after having achieved NVQ level 3.

Find out more

SEMTA, Sector Skills Council for Science, Engineering and Manufacturing Technologies
14 Upton Road, Watford WD18 0JT.
Semta Learning Advice Line: 0800 282 167. www.semta.org.uk

Engineering Council (UK)
246 High Holborn, London WC1V 7EX.
Tel: 020 3206 0500. www.engc.org.uk

Engineering and Technology Board
Address as above.
Tel: 020 3206 0400. www.etechb.co.uk

Science, Technology, Engineering and Mathematics Network (STEMNET)
Address as above.
Tel: 020 3206 0450. www.stemnet.org.uk

The Institution of Engineering and Technology
Michael Faraday House, Stevenage SG1 2AY.
Tel: 01438 313 311. www.theiet.org

Royal Aeronautical Society
4 Hamilton Place, London WIJ 7BQ.
Tel: 020 7670 4300. www.aerosociety.com

Institution of Chemical Engineers
Davis Building, 165-189 Railway Terrace, Rugby CV21 3HQ.
Tel: 01788 578214. www.whynotchemeng.com and www.icheme.org

Institution of Civil Engineers
One Great George Street, London SW1P 3AA.
Tel: 020 7222 7722. www.ice.org.uk

Institution of Structural Engineers
11 Upper Belgrave Street, London SWIX 8BH.
Tel: 020 7235 4535. www.istructe.org

Energy Institute
61 New Cavendish Street, London WIG 7AR.
Tel: 020 7467 7100. www.energyinst.org.uk

Institution of Gas Engineers and Managers
Charnwood Wing, Holywell Park, Ashby Road, Loughborough LE11 3GH.
Tel: 01509 282728. www.igem.org.uk

The Institute of Marine Engineering, Science and Technology
80 Coleman Street, London EC2R 5BJ.
Tel: 020 7382 2600. www.imarest.org

Royal Institution of Naval Architects
10 Upper Belgrave Street, London SW1X 8BQ.
Tel: 020 7235 4622. www.rina.org.uk

Institution of Mechanical Engineers
1 Birdcage Walk, London SW1H 9JJ.
Tel: 020 7222 7899. www.imeche.org

Institute of Materials, Minerals and Mining
Danum House, South Parade, Doncaster DNI 2DY.
Tel: 01302 320486. www.iom3.org

Working in the Built Environment & Construction – published by VT Lifeskills, £8.50. Includes profiles of various civil engineers.

How to Get Ahead in Engineering – published by Heinemann, £12.99.

Engineering Technician – from the *Real Life Guides* series – published by Trotman, £9.99.

Environmental health

Most environmental health officers work for local authorities to ensure a healthy environment for us all. They inspect housing, workplaces, restaurants and shops where food is sold. They monitor levels of air pollution and deal with complaints about excessive noise. Officers need to be persuasive, but persistent, to bring about changes. There are also opportunities in the private sector.

Getting started

- Training is usually through an accredited degree course, followed by a period of practical training. Some courses last four years, allowing you to complete your practical training during a sandwich year.

- To start, you need at least two A levels, or the equivalent, plus supporting GCSEs at grades A*-C. One A level must be in a science subject.

Find out more

Chartered Institute of Environmental Health

Chadwick Court, 15 Hatfields, London SE1 8DJ.
Tel: 020 7928 6006. www.cieh.org/careers

For local government careers information: www.LGcareers.com

Working in the Environment – published by VT Lifeskills, £8.50. Includes a profile of an environmental health practitioner.

Environmental work

Living in a pleasant and safe environment is essential to our wellbeing. There are many areas of work where concern for the environment forms an important part. You can work:

- in scientific research – studying climate change, pollution etc

- in business and industry – e.g. in pest control, waste management, energy supply

- for Government agencies – Natural England, for example, working to manage the countryside and protect the landscape

- for charities and campaigning groups – caring for the environment in a practical way, collecting data etc

- in the media – through working on nature and environment journals, television documentaries etc

Getting started

- Some administration posts require a few good GCSEs to start.

- There are opportunities through Apprenticeships and Advanced Apprenticeships working towards NVQ levels 2 and 3.

- The National Trust offers a three-year Careership training scheme for gardeners and countryside wardens.

- There are countryside management courses at colleges of further education. You may need around four GCSEs at grades A*-C for entry.

- Many posts require degree-level qualifications. Science and geography degrees are useful, especially for research jobs; vocational degree courses lead you into specific careers such as planning or surveying; there are also courses in environmental science/studies.

- If you are interested in a career in environmental work, Diplomas in environmental and land-based studies are being introduced from 2009.

Find out more

The Institution of Environmental Sciences
Suite 7, 38 Ebury Street, London SW1W 0LU.
Tel: 020 7730 5516. www.ies-uk.org.uk

Natural England
The Enquiry Service, Northminster House, Peterborough PE1 1UA.
Tel: 0845 600 3078. www.naturalengland.org.uk

Environment Agency
Rio House, Waterside Drive, Aztec West, Almondsbury, Bristol BS32 4UD.
Tel: 08708 506 506. www.environment-agency.gov.uk

NERC – Natural Environment Research Council
Polaris House, North Star Avenue, Swindon SN2 1EU.
Tel: 01793 411500. www.nerc.ac.uk

Chartered Institute of Water and Environmental Management (CIWEM)
15 John Street, London WC1N 2EB.
Tel: 020 7831 3110. www.ciwem.org
The CIWEM's careers website has job profiles, real-life case studies, university and course information, links to conservation organisations etc: www.environmentalcareers.org.uk

For an idea of the jobs available, view: www.environmentjobs.co.uk

Working in the Environment – published by VT Lifeskills, £8.50.

Estate agency, auctioneering and valuation

- **Estate agents** act for people wishing to sell property – houses, farms, factories, shops and offices. They arrange mortgages and also manage property on behalf of landlords – collecting rents and arranging for repairs to be done.

- **Auctioneers** sell property as well as animals, furniture and secondhand goods.

- **Valuers** assess the value of all types of property for rating, taxation, probate and insurance purposes. They work in local authorities, the Inland Revenue, or for estate agents and auctioneers in private practice.

Getting started

- You can start with no qualifications, perhaps as a receptionist or clerical assistant, and work towards NVQs at levels 2-4 whilst in employment.

- Apprenticeships and Advanced Apprenticeships in property services lead to NVQs at levels 2 and 3.

- If you wish to take your studies to a high level, there are degree courses such as real estate management or property management and investment. There are also courses in art history, and courses run by the major auction houses.

- There are distance- and open-learning courses leading to professional qualifications.

Find out more

The Royal Institution of Chartered Surveyors
Surveyor Court, Westwood Way, Coventry CV4 8JE.
Tel: 0870 333 1600. www.rics.org

National Association of Estate Agents
Arbon House, 6 Tournament Court, Edgehill Drive, Warwick CV34 6LG.
Tel: 01926 496800. www.naea.co.uk

Events management

All events – pop concerts, agricultural shows, sports meetings etc – need managers who can organise all the different aspects of the event and bring them together so that the whole thing runs smoothly. Excellent organisation and problem-solving skills are vital.

Getting started

- There are no set entry requirements. Qualifications in leisure management, tourism, business, marketing etc are obviously useful.

- You can work towards NVQs in events at levels 2 to 4, while you are employed.

- If you want to work at managerial level, there are foundation degree, HND and degree courses in event management.

- If you are interested in a career in events management, a Diploma in business, administration and finance may be available in your school from 2009.

Find out more

Association for Conferences and Events

Riverside House, High Street, Huntingdon PE29 3SG.
Tel: 01480 457595. www.aceinternational.org
You can find details of events management companies on the website.

National Outdoor Events Association

7 Hamilton Way, Wallington, Surrey SM6 9NJ.
Tel: 020 8669 8121. www.noea.org.uk
Links to events companies are on the website.

Working in Marketing, Advertising & PR – published by VT Lifeskills, £8.50. Includes profiles of event organisers.

Exporting

Exporters or international traders arrange for the shipment of British goods, sold to customers from overseas, to anywhere in the world, by means of air or sea transport. They also have to deal with all the paperwork involved – customs, insurance, taxes etc. An exporter may work in an individual company's export department or for a freight forwarding company.

Getting started

- Young people may start through an Apprenticeship or Advanced Apprenticeship, leading to NVQs at levels 2 and 3.

- You can study for qualifications in international trade, offered by the Institute of Export, while you are working. The level of the exams you take depends on your qualifications and experience; you can start at 16 with some good GCSEs.

- There are relevant foundation degree, HND and degree courses – such as in international business.

Find out more

Institute of Export
Export House, Minerva Business Park, Lynch Wood, Peterborough PE2 6FT.
Tel: 01733 404400. www.export.org.uk

Farming and agricultural advisory work

Farming includes the production of livestock – dairy cows, beef cattle, pigs, sheep and poultry, and arable farming (crop production). Agriculture uses around 75% of the land available in the UK. Nowadays, **farmworkers** need to be highly skilled and **farm managers** need to understand business. **Agricultural advisers** offer consultancy, research and laboratory services.

Getting started

- For most courses, you need to have had some practical farming experience before you start.

- There are full-time courses at agricultural colleges. You probably need a few GCSEs at grades A*-C to start. Science subjects are useful.

- There are degree courses in agriculture, agricultural sciences and related subjects for which you need at least two A levels or equivalent, plus supporting GCSEs at grades A*-C. Science subjects are important.

- Consultants, advisers and scientists have degrees. Foundation degrees are also available in land-based subjects.

- Young people can start through Apprenticeships and Advanced Apprenticeships in agricultural crops and livestock. These offer training based with an employer leading to NVQs at levels 2 and 3.

- If you interested in a career in farming, a Diploma in environmental and land-based studies is being introduced from 2009.

Find out more

Lantra
Lantra House, Stoneleigh Park, Near Coventry, Warwickshire CV8 2LG. Helpline: 0845 707 8007. www.lantra.co.uk and www.ajobin.com Contact for details of training and qualifications.

Working in Food & Drink (includes a profile of a dairy farmer) and *Working in the Environment* (includes a profile of an organic farm manager) – both published by VT Lifeskills, £8.50 each.

Farriery: see Horses – careers with

Fashion – clothing production

Most clothes are mass produced in factories. The process from first idea to sales outlet is a long one, and involves design, production – cutting, machining, pressing and examining – engineering and management. Haute couture is the creation of limited edition and hand-made clothes. Bespoke tailoring produces hand-made, high quality clothes for individual customers. Obviously, being interested in design, textiles and fashion is vital.

Getting started

- Basic production jobs, such as machining or pressing, do not require any particular qualifications. Most firms give full training, leading to NVQs.

- Many young people start through Apprenticeships and Advanced Apprenticeships in different aspects of the clothing industry, leading to NVQs at levels 2 and 3 respectively. You may need a few GCSEs at grades A*-C to start an Apprenticeship in a technical subject, such as service engineering.

- Full- or part-time college courses, for which you need GCSEs at grades A*-C in maths and a physical science, are routes for trainee technicians and technologists.

- Specialist college courses offer training in areas such as bespoke tailoring, embroidery etc.

- There are some degree courses in fashion and clothing technology.

- Some 14- to 16-year-olds may have the opportunity to take a Young Apprenticeship in textiles, combining learning and work experience with an employer with study at school and college.

Find out more

Skillfast-UK

www.skillfast-uk.org

Working in Fashion & Clothing – published by VT Lifeskills, £8.50.

Fashion design: see Art and design

Fast-fit work: see Motor vehicle work

Film and video production: see Media: radio, TV, film and video/DVD

Financial advice

Financial advisers help people to choose their mortgages, pensions, investments, savings plans etc. Some are independent and will offer impartial advice and sell products from a range of suppliers; some are tied to a bank, building society or insurance company and only sell their company's products. Some financial advisers specialise in tax advice work. You need to be good with numbers and have excellent people skills.

Getting started

- There are no minimum formal educational requirements to start training. Employers set their own, which can vary from GCSEs to A levels or even a degree.

- You will need to pass professional exams before you can give financial advice to clients.

- Training is usually work-based. There is an Advanced Apprenticeship in advising on financial products, leading to NVQ 3.

- Some schools offer the *ifs School of Finance* Certificate/ Diploma in Financial Studies.

- Trainee tax advisers may have higher-level qualifications, perhaps an HND or a degree.

- If you are interested in a career in finance, Diplomas in business, administration and finance are being introduced from 2009.

Find out more

The Personal Finance Society
42-48 High Road, South Woodford, London E18 2JP.
Tel: 020 8530 0852. www.thepfs.org

The Association of Taxation Technicians
12 Upper Belgrave Street, London SW1X 8BB.
Tel: 020 7235 2544. www.att.org.uk

For information about *ifs School of Finance* qualifications, look at: www.ifslearning.ac.uk

Working in Advice & Counselling – published by VT Lifeskills, £8.50. Includes profiles of a money adviser and an independent financial adviser.

Fine art: see Art and design

Firefighting

Firefighters not only fight fires and save lives, they deal with all types of emergency, such as road accidents and the spillage of dangerous chemicals. In these situations, you need to be able to keep cool in a crisis. Firefighters also inspect buildings to make sure that they comply with fire safety regulations and instruct members of the public in fire safety.

Getting started

- Each local fire and rescue service is responsible for its own recruitment, but there are national psychological, physical and medical tests for applicants.

- Firefighters need to be strong and fit, with good teamwork and communication skills.

- You can apply with any level of qualifications.

- Applicants with disabilities are assessed individually to see if they can perform the duties of a firefighter.

- You must be at least 18.

- Training takes place at a local or regional training centre as well as at your local fire station.

- If you are interested in a career with the fire service, Diplomas in public services are being introduced from 2010.

Find out more

Contact your local **fire and rescue service headquarters** (the address will be in the local telephone directory).

There is information about firefighter careers on: www.fire.gov.uk/careers

The Fire Service – from the *Real Life Guides* series – published by Trotman, £9.99.

Working in Police, Fire & Security – published by VT Lifeskills, £8.50.

Fitness instructing: see Sports and fitness instructing

Food science and technology

Food scientists study the chemistry and biology of foods from raw materials through processing to the final product. **Food technologists** use food science and other technological know-how to turn raw materials into finished products for the consumer. Besides jobs in the huge food industry, there are opportunities in research and in local and national government departments such as environmental health and the Food Standards Agency. Food scientists are in demand!

Getting started

- Young people can start through Apprenticeships or Advanced Apprenticeships, which lead to NVQs at levels 2 and 3 respectively. You may need a few GCSEs, including sciences, to start.

- At **technician level**, you can work towards NVQs whilst in employment.

- There are some relevant BTEC National courses in applied science which are useful for technician-level jobs. To start, you normally need the equivalent of four GCSEs at grades A*-C including science and maths, and a subject demonstrating the use of English.

- Most **food scientists and technologists** have foundation degrees, HNDs or, more likely, degrees. There are courses in food science and food technology, but you could start by studying another branch of science, such as chemistry. You may be expected to have science A levels, or the equivalent, to start a higher education course, plus supporting GCSEs.

Find out more

Institute of Food Science and Technology
5 Cambridge Court, 210 Shepherd's Bush Road, London W6 7NJ.
Tel: 020 7603 6316. www.foodtechcareers.org

Improve Ltd (Food and Drink Sector Skills Council)
Ground Floor, Providence House, 2 Innovation Close, Heslington, York YO10 5ZF.
Tel: 0845 644 0448. www.improveltd.co.uk

Working in Food & Drink – published by VT Lifeskills, £8.50. Includes a profile of a senior scientist.

Footcare assistance: see Podiatry

Forensic science

Forensic scientists work closely with the police to help solve crimes against people and property. They use different scientific disciplines to test and analyse material. A lot of the work takes place in a laboratory, although they may have to visit scenes of crime. You would be faced with some unpleasant sights during the course of this work, so it's important not to be squeamish. The work isn't always as exciting as it looks in TV programmes, but it can be crucial in solving crimes. Entry is very competitive.

Getting started

- You'll need an understanding of – and preferably experience in – chemistry and biology laboratory work.

- To train as an assistant forensic scientist, you need a minimum of four GCSEs (including English and maths or a science), plus at least one science A level.

- Forensic scientists have degrees in a chemistry- or biology-based science. Many have postgraduate qualifications.

Find out more

The Forensic Science Service Headquarters
Trident Court, 2920 Solihull Parkway, Birmingham Business Park, Birmingham B37 7YN.
Tel: 0121 329 5200. www.forensic.gov.uk

The Forensic Science Society
18a Mount Parade, Harrogate, North Yorkshire HG1 1BX.
Tel: 01423 506068. www.forensic-science-society.org.uk

Working in Science – published by VT Lifeskills, £8.50. Includes profiles of a crime scene examiner and a DNA analyst.

Forestry

Forestry work is about managing forests, and includes planting, tending, felling and the preparation and marketing of timber. About half the area of productive woodland in the UK is privately owned; the rest is managed for the nation, by Forest Enterprise, part of the Forestry Commission. The work also involves arboriculture and tree surgery – managing and maintaining woodland areas for amenity, leisure and conservation purposes.

Getting started

- Many young people start as **forest workers** or trainee craftspeople through work-based learning, such as an Apprenticeship in trees and timber, working towards NVQs.

- Forest workers or trainee craftspeople need no formal qualifications to start, but some colleges may ask for a few GCSEs, or the equivalent, before you start on a course.

- To work as a **forester** or **forest officer** you need to have an HND or a degree in forestry. A degree course may ask for a science A level and, perhaps, a year of practical experience.

- If you are interested in a career in forestry, Diplomas in environmental and land-based studies are being introduced from 2009.

Find out more

The Forestry Commission
231 Corstorphine Road, Edinburgh EH12 7AT.
Tel: 0131 334 0303. www.forestry.gov.uk

Lantra
Lantra House, Stoneleigh Park, Nr Coventry, Warwickshire CV8 2LG.
Helpline: 0845 707 8007. www.lantra.co.uk and www.ajobin.com

Working in the Environment – published by VT Lifeskills, £8.50. Includes a profile of a forest craftsperson.

Freight forwarding: see Logistics and transport

Fuel technology: see Engineering

Funeral work

Funeral directors make funeral arrangements, making sure that all the legal requirements are met. **Embalmers** prepare bodies for burial or cremation. **Cemetery and graveyard workers** administer cremations and burials and manage the premises and the grounds. Compassion and understanding are important qualities for this kind of work.

Getting started

- You do not need any formal qualifications to start working, but a few GCSEs may be expected. Your manner and way of dealing with people are more important.

- There are work-based courses leading to qualifications at three levels: the Foundation Certificate in Funeral Service (for operatives and assistants), the Diploma in Funeral Directing for which you need at least two years' work experience, and the Diploma in Funeral Service Management.

- It's possible to take a foundation degree in funeral services through distance learning.

- Co-operative Funeralcare, with branches all over the country, offers training to its employees, leading to its own BTEC qualification.

- You can study to become an embalmer while you are working, or through a correspondence course. There are a few full-time courses.

Find out more

National Association of Funeral Directors
618 Warwick Road, Solihull, West Midlands B91 1AA.
Tel: 0845 230 1343. www.nafd.org.uk
Produces the booklet, *The Funeral Service as a Career* – available to download from the website.

British Institute of Embalmers
21c Station Road, Knowle, Solihull, West Midlands B93 0HL.
Tel: 01564 778991. www.bioe.co.uk

Furniture design: see Art and design

Gardening: see Horticulture

Gas engineering: see Engineering

General practitioner (GP): see Medicine and surgery

Genetics

Genetics is the study of genes. Genes are the working parts of DNA – that's the chemical database which makes humans, plants, animals, insects and micro-organisms what they are. Geneticists help to diagnose and treat disease, modify crops and farm animals, develop antibiotics and conserve endangered species. The work is laboratory-based.

Getting started

- You can train as a **laboratory technician** through an Apprenticeship or Advanced Apprenticeship, working towards NVQs at levels 2 and 3 respectively. To begin training, you are likely to need GCSEs at grades A*-C, including maths and science.

- **Geneticists** have degrees. You can take a degree in a relevant subject like biology or biochemistry, or a degree in genetics. You need science A levels or the equivalent to start.

- Most research posts will require further study.

Find out more

Institute of Biology
9 Red Lion Court, London EC4A 3EF.
Tel: 020 7936 5900. www.iob.org

The Physiological Society
Peer House, Verulam Street, London WC1X 8LZ.
Tel: 020 7269 5710. www.physoc.org

Information about careers in genetics can be found on the **Genetics Society** website: www.genetics.org.uk

Geology

Geologists study the structure, evolution and composition of the Earth and the natural mineral and energy resources that it contains. Geologists work in the field, carrying out ground surveys for projects involved with the exploration and production of fuels, metals, construction materials and groundwater; construction, planning and land utilisation and caring for our environment. They also analyse and identify materials in the laboratory. The oil, gas, water, mining/quarrying and construction industries are the main employers. There are opportunities overseas.

Getting started

- With GCSEs at grades A*-C, and preferably science A levels or the equivalent, you can work as a **technician**.

- **Geologists** have degrees. There are relevant degrees in geology, geoscience and earth sciences, as well as in more specialised subjects, such as geophysics. You need science A levels (not necessarily geography or geology), or the equivalent, to start a course.

Find out more

British Geological Survey
Kingsley Dunham Centre, Keyworth, Nottingham NG12 5GG.
Tel: 0115 936 3143. www.bgs.ac.uk

The Geological Society
Burlington House, Piccadilly, London WIJ 0BG.
Tel: 020 7434 9944. www.geolsoc.org.uk

Glazier work: see Building crafts

Graphic design: see Art and design

Hairdressing

Hairdressers cut, shampoo, set, style, colour, straighten and perm hair. Sometimes this career is combined with beauty therapy. You need to be a sociable person and to take care of your own appearance, as you are a walking advert for your place of work! Skin conditions or breathing problems could make this work difficult for you.

Getting started

- You don't need any formal qualifications to start training. You learn on the job, and perhaps go to college part time. Some salons and college courses may ask for GCSEs.

- Most training for young people is through Apprenticeships and Advanced Apprenticeships, leading to NVQs at levels 2 and 3.

- The other main way to train is through a full-time course at a college of further education, also leading to NVQs at levels 2 and 3. You may need some GCSEs – sciences are useful.

- There are some private hairdressing schools. Their courses can be expensive.

- There are higher education courses in salon management.

- Some 14- to 16-year-olds may have the opportunity to take a Young Apprenticeship in hairdressing, combining learning and work experience with an employer with study at school and college.

- If you are interested in a career in hairdressing, Diplomas in hair and beauty studies are being introduced from 2009.

Find out more

Habia
Oxford House, Sixth Avenue, Sky Business Park, Robin Hood Airport, Doncaster DN9 3GG.
Tel: 0845 230 6080. www.habia.org
Contact for information about careers, qualifications and training.

Hairdressing – from the *Real Life Guides* series – published by Trotman, £9.99.

Working in Work Experience & Volunteering – published by VT Lifeskills, £8.50. Includes a profile of a hairdressing assistant.

Health and safety work: see Safety work

Health visiting: see Nursing

Heating and ventilation: see Building services engineering

Herbalism: see Complementary medicine

Homoeopathy: see Complementary medicine

Horses – careers with

Grooms work in stables, pony trekking centres etc caring for the horses, while **riding instructors** teach children and adults to ride; many people combine the two. **Stable lads** (male or female!), **jockeys** and **trainers** work in horseracing. There are also opportunities for **horse breeders**. **Farriers** use blacksmithing skills to fit horseshoes.

Getting started

- Young people can get started in a range of careers working with horses through an Apprenticeship or Advanced Apprenticeship, working towards NVQs at levels 2 and 3. NVQs offer practical work-based training in horse care (levels 1 and 2) and horse care and management (level 3).

- To qualify as a **riding instructor**, you can take exams of the British Horse Society (BHS) or the Association of British Riding Schools (ABRS). There are also college courses available.

- The BHS and the ABRS also offer **grooms'** qualifications.

- You can train to work in **horse breeding**, possibly through an Apprenticeship, at The National Stud.

- If you want to **work with racehorses**, you must complete a recognised training course, e.g. through the British Racing School or the Northern Racing College. You can go on to be a **head lad**, **yard manager**, **trainer** or, if you show special ability – and are the right size! – a **jockey**.

- **Farriery** is skilled work. An Advanced Apprenticeship takes over four years and leads to NVQ level 3 in farriery. You'll need a minimum of four GCSEs at grades A*-C (or the equivalent) to start.

- There are a number of courses in universities and colleges – equine science, horse management etc – which can lead to qualifications, such as a foundation degree, HND or degree.

Find out more

British Horse Society (BHS)
Stoneleigh Deer Park, Kenilworth, Warwickshire CV8 2XZ.
Tel: 08701 202244. www.bhs.org.uk

Association of British Riding Schools (ABRS)
Queen's Chambers, 38-40 Queen Street, Penzance TR18 4BH.
Tel: 01736 369440. www.abrs-info.org

The Farriery Training Agency
Sefton House, Adam Court, Newark Road, Peterborough PEI 5PP.
Tel: 01733 319770. www.farrier-reg.gov.uk

The National Stud
Newmarket, Suffolk CB8 0XE.
Tel: 01638 663464. www.nationalstud.co.uk

British Horseracing Education and Standards Trust (BHEST)
Suite 16, Unit 8, Kings Court, Willie Snaith Road, Newmarket, CB8 7SG.
Tel: 01638 560743. www.bhest.co.uk

Lantra
Lantra House, Stoneleigh Park, Nr Coventry, Warwickshire CV8 2LG.
Helpline: 0845 707 8007. www.lantra.co.uk www.ajobin.com

Working with Animals & Wildlife – from the *Real Life Guides series*
published by Trotman, £9.99.

Horticultural therapy: see Creative therapies

Horticulture

There are two main types of horticulture. **Commercial horticulture** is growing fruit, vegetables and flowers as commercial crops, or as seeds and plants for sale in nurseries and garden centres. **Amenity horticulture** involves work in parks and gardens, design and landscaping, and the maintenance of sports grounds and golf courses.

Getting started

- You can attend a full-time college course (mainly at colleges of agriculture and horticulture) for BTEC and other qualifications in horticulture. You normally need four GCSEs at grades A*-C for entry.

- The Royal Horticultural Society (RHS) also awards its own qualifications, run through colleges, including the RHS Certificate, the RHS Advanced Certificate and the RHS Diploma.

- You can start training with an employer, gaining qualifications through a part-time college course. Many young people train through Apprenticeships or Advanced Apprenticeships, leading to NVQs at levels 2 and 3 respectively. Good GCSEs are useful for entry.

- If you want to continue with full-time study, there are foundation degree, HND and degree courses in horticulture and related subjects. You need two A levels (usually including biology and/or chemistry), or the equivalent, for degree course entry, and you may need some previous practical experience.

- The School of Horticulture at the Royal Botanic Gardens at Kew offers a three-year Kew Diploma course in horticulture, equivalent to a degree.

- The National Trust's Careership scheme in amenity horticulture is a three-year, salaried apprenticeship, leading to NVQ level 3. You need four GCSEs at grades A*-C to start.

- If you are interested in a career in horticulture, Diplomas in environmental and land-based studies are being introduced from 2009.

Find out more

Institute of Horticulture
Institute of Biology, 9 Red Lion Court, London EC4A 3EF.
Tel: 020 7936 5957. www.horticulture.org.uk

Lantra
Lantra House, Stoneleigh Park, Nr Coventry, Warwickshire CV8 2LG.
Helpline: 0845 707 8007. www.lantra.co.uk and www.ajobin.com

Royal Horticultural Society
Education Department, Wisley, Woking, Surrey GU23 6QB.
Tel: 0845 260 5000. www.rhs.org.uk/learning/education/careers
Job profiles and *Come into horticulture* can be downloaded from the website above.

Institute of Groundsmanship
28 Stratford Office Village, Walker Avenue, Wolverton Mill East, Milton Keynes MK12 5TW.
Tel: 01908 312511. www.iog.org

Landscape Institute
33 Great Portland Street, London W1W 8QG.
Tel: 020 7299 4500. www.landscapeinstitute.org

The National Trust
Heelis, Kemble Drive, Swindon SN2 2NA.
Tel: 01793 817400. www.nationaltrust.org.uk and
www.skilledfutures.org.uk

School of Horticulture, Royal Botanic Gardens
Kew, Richmond, Surrey TW9 3AB.
Tel: 020 8332 5545. www.rbgkew.org.uk/education/diploma

Working in the Environment – published by VT Lifeskills, £8.50.

Hospitality: see Catering and hospitality

Hotels: see Catering and hospitality

Housing management

Housing managers work for housing organisations, including local authorities, housing charities and trusts. They are responsible for organising the planning, construction, allocation and upkeep of rented properties. They must know about the structure of buildings, landlord and tenant law, and planning.

Getting started

- You can start in an administrative/support post in a housing department with GCSEs, or the equivalent, and work towards NVQs at levels 2-4.

- The Chartered Institute of Housing offers its own qualifications.

- There are Apprenticeships and Advanced Apprenticeships for young people, leading to NVQ levels 2 and 3 respectively.

- There are a number of full- and part-time foundation degrees, Higher National qualifications and degrees in housing studies and housing management.

Find out more

Chartered Institute of Housing
Octavia House, Westwood Way, Coventry CV4 8JP.
Tel: 024 7685 1749. www.cih.org

Asset Skills – the Sector Skills Council for housing.
Tel: 08000 567 160. www.assetskills.org

National Housing Federation
Lion Court, 25 Procter Street, London WC1V 6NY.
Tel: 020 7067 1010. www.housing.org.uk
The body representing the independent social housing sector.

For information on jobs in local government housing: www.LGjobs.com

Human resource management

Human resource managers plan staffing levels, recruit and select staff, run training programmes and negotiate with trades unions about pay and working conditions. They work in local authorities, hospitals and higher education institutions, as well as in commercial and industrial concerns.

Getting started

- You can work your way up by joining a human resources department in a clerical or secretarial post, and studying part time. You may need good GCSEs or A levels (or the equivalent) to start. One part-time study route leads to the Chartered Institute of Personnel and Development's (CIPD) Certificate in Personnel Practice for which there are no specific entry requirements.

- Young people can start through an Advanced Apprenticeship, leading to NVQ 3.

- In most organisations, human resource management is a career for graduates (or at least holders of foundation degrees or HNDs) as it is seen as part of general management.

- NVQs at levels 2-5 are awarded by the CIPD. You gain NVQs by assessment in the workplace.

Find out more

Chartered Institute of Personnel and Development (CIPD)
151 The Broadway, London SW19 1JQ.
Tel: 020 8612 6200. www.cipd.co.uk

ICT: see **Information and communication technology**

Industrial design: see **Art and design**

Information and communication technology

Most people use computers as part of their working life, but specialists in ICT are needed to design and maintain the computer systems we all rely on. Job titles and descriptions vary, but the following is a rough guide.

- **Systems analysts and designers** need to understand and interpret the way an organisation operates, in order to design a suitable computer system.

- **Systems programmers or developers** write or develop the programs that operate the computer systems in computing languages. They need to think in a logical way.

- **Software engineers** are involved in the whole process of developing ICT systems – so need a technical understanding of both the computer hardware (machinery) and the software – the programs.

- **Technical support staff** provide help to users who are having problems with the computer software or hardware they are using. They may be based at a helpdesk, advising people over the phone or, if dealing with hardware problems, they may visit clients.

- **Computer engineers** research, design and develop computer equipment, and are involved in its manufacture. They work as part of a team with other specialists in engineering and ICT.

- **Database managers** look after an organisation's databases, which may contain information on customers, orders, financial information and so on. The work includes making sure there are good back-up and security systems, training staff to use the systems, sorting out problems and developing the systems for the future.

- **Website designers** find out what the client needs, and then develop the website according to the client's brief. Website designers need a knowledge of interactive programming languages, as well as creative ability and imagination.

- **Multimedia/interactive computer systems** use text, sound, still or moving images and graphics. They are developed for various purposes including for entertainment (e.g. computer games), for education and training, or for design work. People from a range of backgrounds – such as electronics engineers, musicians and film animators – work together to develop multimedia systems.

Getting started

- Look carefully at the various courses on offer – there is a huge range available including GCSEs/applied GCSEs and AS/A levels/ applied AS/A levels, BTEC First and Nationals, OCR Nationals and City & Guilds courses in ICT/computing.

- If you are interested in a career in ICT, Diplomas in information technology may be available; for careers in interactive media, Diplomas in creative and media may be relevant.

- Higher Apprenticeships are available combining higher education with employment.

- For entry to **programming**, a foundation degree, HND or degree is usually required – not necessarily in computing. **Systems analysts** are usually experienced programmers.

- For **software engineering**, a relevant degree is usually required.

- Entry qualifications for **technical support** staff vary, from entry with GCSEs and training with an employer, through to entry with a relevant degree. Young people can get started in technical support through an Apprenticeship or Advanced Apprenticeship.

- **Computer engineers** need a degree in a specialist subject such as electronic engineering or computer engineering. Those with a foundation degree or HND may qualify as engineers with further study.

- **Database managers** usually have previous experience in some aspect of computing, or, occasionally, new computing graduates may be employed.

- There are no set entry routes into **website design** work, but employers look for those with relevant training or experience – some enter from a design background, and others from a computing background.

- People working in **multimedia** have a wide range of backgrounds, some creative and others computing-related. There are a number of multimedia degree courses available, which offer a starting point.

- Once employed, you will usually work towards further qualifications, including NVQs, and/or qualifications offered by professional bodies.

Find out more

e-skills UK
1 Castle Lane, London SW1E 6DR.
Tel: 0207 963 8920. www.e-skills.com

Information & Communications Technology – from the *Real Life Guides* series – published by Trotman, £9.99.

Information science: see Library and information science and management

---

Insurance

Insurance is divided into two main areas: **general insurance**, where individuals or organisations take out insurance to protect themselves against accident, fire, theft and so on, and **life insurance**, where people insure themselves against dying early, or being permanently injured.

Insurance is a major industry. Jobs include:

- **underwriters** – who assess the insurance risk and work out the terms and conditions of insurance policies

- **claims staff** – including claims technicians, claims negotiators and loss adjustors, who deal with claims made by customers

- **brokers** – who acts as the link between the customer and the insurance company

- **insurance surveyors** – who inspect buildings, ships etc that are to be insured

- **actuaries** – statistical experts who work out how much we should be paying for life insurance (see *Actuarial work*).

Getting started

- Young people may enter through an Apprenticeship or Advanced Apprenticeship, which provides training with an employer, leading to NVQs at levels 2 and 3 respectively.

- You can look for a clerical or technician-level job – employers may ask for four GCSEs at grades A*-C or perhaps two A levels – and work your way up by studying part time for professional qualifications.

- There are training schemes for graduates in all areas of work.

- The Chartered Insurance Institute's qualifications include a Certificate that requires no particular entry qualifications, an Advanced Diploma that requires at least two A levels or equivalent and higher-level qualifications for graduates.

- The *ifs* offers qualifications from a level 3 Certificate to degree-level qualifications.

- If you are interested in a career in insurance, Diplomas in business, administration and finance are being introduced from 2009.

Find out more

Chartered Insurance Institute
Careers Information Service, 20 Aldermanbury, London EC2V 7HY.
Tel: 020 7417 4415. www.cii.co.uk

ifs **School of Finance**
IFS House, 4-9 Burgate Lane, Canterbury CT1 2XJ.
Tel: 01227 818609. www.ifslearning.ac.uk

Interior design: see Art and design

Interpreting: see Language work

Investment analysis and fund management

Investment analysts provide advice to stockbrokers and fund managers wishing to buy shares and make other investments. Investment analysts need a good knowledge and understanding of the issues that affect investment markets, in order to try to predict future performance. Employers include banks and building societies, stockbroking firms and pensions funds.

Investment fund managers are responsible for managing funds, such as pension and life assurance funds, which may be worth billions of pounds.

Getting started

- You must first get a degree – preferably, but not necessarily, in a subject such as economics, statistics or business

- This should be followed by part-time study leading to professional qualifications, such as that of Chartered Financial Analyst.

Find out more

UK Society of Investment Professionals
4th Floor, 90 Basinghall Street, London EC2V 5AY.
Tel: 020 7796 3000. www.uksip.org

IT: see Information and communication technology

Jewellery making: see Art and design

Journalism

Journalists work on newspapers, magazines, radio, television and online. They work as reporters, as feature writers producing articles on special topics, as specialists in areas such as sport or business topics and as sub-editors. Entry is extremely competitive. Apart from the necessary academic qualifications, applicants need to show an interest in journalism, perhaps by having written articles for school or community publications.

Journalists need good communication skills, determination and persistence, and must be able to work to strict deadlines! Evening and weekend work is always part of the job.

Getting started

- One-year, full-time, pre-entry courses in journalism are offered at various colleges. You need two A levels or equivalent, plus five GCSEs at grades A*-C, including English. Many applicants have degrees. There is also a distance-learning pre-entry course. After a course you need to find a job with a training contract.

- About a quarter of journalists enter directly into a job with a local or regional paper, and train and study whilst working. Although the minimum entry qualifications for direct entry are five GCSEs at grades A*-C, including English, nearly all recruits have A levels or a degree.

- A few large employers, including broadcasting companies, provide in-house training schemes.

- At higher-education level, there are a number of foundation degree, HND and degree courses accredited by the National Council for the Training of Journalists or the Periodicals Training Council. After finding a job with a paper or magazine, you follow a training programme.

- Graduates of other subjects may follow a one-year postgraduate journalism course, before finding employment. There are also 20-week 'fast-track' pre-entry courses for graduates. A degree in media studies does not, on its own, provide training for a career in journalism.

- If you are interested in a career in journalism, Diplomas in creative and media may be available.

Find out more

National Council for the Training of Journalists
The New Granary, Station Road, Newport, Saffron Walden, Essex CB11 3PL.
Tel: 01799 544014. www.nctj.com

The Periodicals Training Council
Queens House, Lincoln's Inn Fields, London WC2A 3LJ.
Tel: 020 7400 7570. www.ppa.co.uk/cgi-bin/wms.pl/175
The careers guide, *Your Future in Magazines*, can be viewed online.

Working in English and *Working in Work Experience & Volunteering* – both published by VT Lifeskills, £8.50 each.

Journalism Uncovered – published by Trotman, £12.99.

Laboratory technician work

Laboratory technicians and assistants prepare and maintain the equipment in a scientific laboratory, and set up experiments. They may take readings, mix chemical solutions, prepare slides and undertake routine experiments. Laboratory staff are employed in industry (from pharmaceutical firms to food manufacturers), in government-funded research institutes and agencies, in schools, colleges and universities and in medical laboratories (see *Biomedical science*).

Getting started

- Employers usually prefer applicants with GCSEs at grades A*-C, including English, maths and science, or equivalent. GCSE in applied science is also relevant. Some employers look for entrants with level 3 qualifications, such as A levels or the equivalent.

- Once employed, training is usually through part-time study, perhaps leading to BTEC or City & Guilds qualifications, or to qualifications of The Institute of Science Technology. NVQs can be gained in the workplace.

- You may be able to train through an Advanced Apprenticeship leading to NVQ level 3.

Find out more

IST – The Institute of Science Technology
Kingfisher House, 90 Rockingham Street, Sheffield S1 4EB.
Tel: 0114 276 3197. www.istonline.org.uk

Working in Science – published by VT Lifeskills, £8.50.

Land surveying: see Surveying

Landscape architecture

Landscape architects design the layout of open spaces such as parks and playgrounds, or the land surrounding public buildings, hospitals, hotels and businesses. They may also work on land reclamation schemes and new housing developments. Their work includes designing the hard surfacing – paving, paths etc – as well as all the planting on the site. They discuss with their client what he/she wants, produce plans and designs, work out costs and then oversee the work in progress.

Two closely related career areas are **landscape management**, which involves the long-term management and development of landscape schemes, and **landscape science**, which is concerned with the biological aspects of a designed landscape.

Getting started

- You can take a degree in landscape architecture; for entry you need at least two A levels – art, biology and geography are relevant – or equivalent qualifications, plus supporting GCSEs at grades A*-C.

- Alternatively, you can take a degree in a related subject, such as planning, horticulture or architecture, followed by postgraduate study in landscape architecture.

- Once employed, further study and experience leads to membership of The Landscape Institute.

Find out more

The Landscape Institute
33 Great Portland Street, London W1W 8QG.
Tel: 020 7299 4500. www.landscapeinstitute.org.uk

There is a list of relevant courses and careers information on their website.

Working in the Environment – published by VT Lifeskills, £8.50. Includes a profile of a landscape manager.

Language work

Translators translate written material, generally into their own language. Most translators work in a particular field – such as finance, science, engineering or law. In addition to their language skills, translators must have knowledge of the vocabulary used in their specialist area. **Interpreters** can work as:

- conference interpreters at high-level conferences, international meetings and so on, translating speeches into their own language

- liaison interpreters translating into and out of two, or sometimes three, languages being used in a discussion or business meeting

- court interpreters in the law courts

- public service interpreters helping non-English speakers to communicate with public officials and others working in the community. They work with health and social services, police, the UK Border Agency, advice agencies and so on.

Bilingual/trilingual secretaries work in commercial firms or with international bodies. Their duties may include translating letters and documents, typing letters or reports in foreign languages, taking phone calls from abroad, making foreign travel arrangements and so on.

Other careers where languages are useful or essential include teaching foreign languages, travel and tourism, hospitality and catering, the Civil Service (e.g. Diplomatic Service, Ministry of Defence) and in industry and commerce – particularly in export and marketing departments.

Getting started

- **Translators and interpreters** generally need a degree in a modern foreign language, a degree that includes translating or interpreting or perhaps a degree combining languages and another subject. They also usually hold a postgraduate qualification in translating or interpreting. Interpreters preferably need fluency in two foreign languages, and need to be very familiar with the culture of those countries. People who have been brought up as bilingual may find work without the above qualifications.

- To become a **bilingual secretary**, you obviously need good secretarial skills, together with foreign language skills, usually to at least A level standard. A few colleges offer specialist courses.

Find out more

Institute of Translation and Interpreting
Fortuna House, South Fifth Street, Milton Keynes MK9 2EU.
Tel: 01908 325250. www.iti.org.uk
Publishes the leaflets *Getting into Translating* and *Getting into Interpreting*, which can be viewed on the website.

Working in Cultural Heritage – published by VT Lifeskills, £8.50. Includes a profile of an interpreter.

Legal executive work: see Legal work

Legal work

Barristers

Barristers present cases in court. They must gain a thorough understanding of the case beforehand by reading reports, witness statements and, possibly, by talking to the client. Barristers must have a very high intellect, and a good command of language. Barristers are also often consulted for their opinion on legal matters. Clients cannot approach a barrister direct; they must do so through a solicitor. Some barristers are employed in commerce, industry and government departments.

Getting started

- It takes from five to seven years to qualify. You first need a good honours degree in law or in another subject; graduates with non-law degrees must undertake a one-year conversion course. Normally, three A levels at high grades (subjects are rarely specified) or equivalent qualifications, plus supporting

GCSEs (including English) are required for entry to a law degree.

- Everyone intending to practise at the Bar of England and Wales must then follow the Bar Vocational Course (BVC); students must join one of the four Inns of Court before starting the BVC, and have to attend a number of qualifying sessions at their Inn. Finally, a newly-qualified barrister must spend a year as a pupil with an experienced barrister. Competition is very stiff for entry to each stage of training.

Solicitors

Solicitors carry out a wide range of legal work and normally act on the instructions of clients. Clients can ask for any legal service, from buying a home to selling a company. A solicitor's role is to give legal advice and representation, and matters can vary from crime to conveyancing (house buying and selling), from making a will to carrying out a multimillion pound deal. Generally solicitors represent their clients in the lower courts, and, in certain circumstances, in the higher courts, but usually a barrister is engaged for this.

Getting started

- Training takes at least six years. You can start by taking a law degree, and then complete two further stages – a Legal Practice Course, and then a two-year training contract in a solicitor's office or other approved organisation. (See under *Barrister* above for entry qualifications for a law degree.)

- Alternatively, you could choose to do a degree in a subject other than law and then complete a one-year, full-time, or two-year, part-time 'conversion' course before going on the Legal Practice Course.

- It's possible to qualify as a solicitor after working as a fully-qualified legal executive.

Legal executives

Legal executives work in solicitors' offices and legal departments and usually specialise in a particular area of work – family law, litigation (taking cases to court), conveyancing, or wills and probate (dealing with matters when someone dies). They prepare documents, do research, interview clients and so on. Some court work can be involved. Legal executives may take on caseloads of their own.

Getting started

- Four GCSEs at grades A*-C, including English, or equivalent qualifications, are the minimum needed to start the training scheme, administered by the Institute of Legal Executives. Study is usually on a part-time or distance-learning basis, while you are employed. Successful completion of the level 3 and level 4 exams, together with five years' experience, leads to qualification as a Fellow of the Institute, which you need to call yourself a legal executive.

- Students without four GCSEs can take the Vocational Legal Studies qualification, which gives entry to the legal executive training programme.

Paralegals

Paralegals deal with many aspects of the law without being qualified lawyers. Some duties may be routine, while others carry considerable responsibility. Paralegals may specialise in one or two areas of the law such as conveyancing, company law or family matters. They may work in solicitors' offices, in industry and commerce and in the public sector.

Getting started

- The National Association of Licensed Paralegals offers part-time and distance-learning courses for members. Minimum entry requirements for the Higher Certificate in Paralegal Studies are five GCSEs at grades A*-C, including English, or equivalent qualifications.

- The Institute of Legal Executives offers flexible training programmes for paralegal work (ILEXPP). The ILEXPP level 2 Certificate in Vocational Paralegal Studies and the level 3 Diploma can be gained through part-time and distance learning courses. There are no formal entry requirements although grade A*-C in English is desirable.

Licensed conveyancers

Licensed conveyancers undertake the legal and administrative work involved in the buying and selling of property – a house, flat or piece of land.

Getting started

- With four GCSEs at grades A*-C, including English, you can start studying for the professional qualification of the Council for Licensed Conveyancers, through part-time or distance-learning study whilst working.

- Two years of supervised practical training is necessary before you can apply for your first licence – a limited licence – and then a further three years' experience before applying for a full licence.

Legal support work

- **Legal secretaries** and PAs (personal assistants) deal with the secretarial and general administrative work in legal offices. Some specialist legal secretarial courses are available.

- **Legal cashiers** are employed by solicitors to look after the office accounts and financial affairs, and the accounts held on behalf of clients, such as trust funds. They may study for exams of the Institute of Legal Cashiers and Administrators.

- **Law costs draftsmen** make sure clients are charged fair fees, and prepare legal bills. They may study for exams of the Association of Law Cost Draftsmen.

- **Outdoor clerks** are employed by large firms of solicitors to undertake general duties, including delivering claims and summonses and attending court to pay fees, fixing dates for court hearings. Training is on the job.

Find out more

Bar Standards Board
289-293 High Holborn, London WC1V 7HZ.
Tel: 020 7611 1444. www.barstandardsboard.org.uk

The Law Society of England and Wales
113 Chancery Lane, London WC2A 1PL.
Tel: 0870 606 2555. www.lawsociety.org.uk

Institute of Legal Executives (ILEX)
Kempston Manor, Kempston, Bedford MK42 7AB.
Tel: 01234 841000. www.ilex.org.uk
For information on ILEX Paralegal Programmes see: www.ilexpp.co.uk

Council for Licensed Conveyancers
16 Glebe Road, Chelmsford, Essex CM 1 1QG.
Tel: 01245 349599. www.theclc.gov.uk

The Institute of Legal Secretaries and PAs/The National Association of Licensed Paralegals
9 Unity Street, Bristol BS1 5HH.
Tel: 0117 927 7007. www.institutelegalsecretaries.com
www.nationalparalegals.co.uk

The Institute of Legal Cashiers and Administrators
2nd Floor, Marlowe House, 109 Station Road, Sidcup, Kent DA15 7ET.
Tel: 020 8302 2867. www.ilca.org.uk

Association of Law Costs Draftsmen
Education Department, 52 Station Road, Woburn Sands, Milton Keynes K17 8RU.
Tel: 01908 282892. www.alcd.org.uk

Working in English – published by VT Lifeskills, £8.50. Includes a profile of a barrister.

Working in Advice & Counselling – published by VT Lifeskills, £8.50. Includes a profile of a solicitor.

Law Uncovered – published by Trotman, £12.99.

Leisure management

Leisure managers look after the running of sports and leisure facilities, which may be owned by local authorities, commercial companies or educational institutions. Facilities range from small sports halls, through to large recreation and leisure centres which may include swimming pools, a bowling alley, ice rink and arts facilities. See also *Sports and fitness instructing* for information about non-management-level work.

Getting started

- There are a variety of routes into leisure management. It is still possible to work your way up from a junior level through part-time study, e.g. by taking qualifications offered by the Institute of Leisure and Amenity Management or the Institute of Sport and Recreation Management.

- Increasingly, entrants to trainee management positions hold higher education qualifications. There is a range of foundation degree, HND and degree courses in leisure management/ sport and recreation management and related subjects. Once employed, entrants continue to study for further professional qualifications on a part-time basis.

- An alternative route is to study a degree in any subject, followed by a postgraduate course in leisure management.

- Experience of organising sporting events and having the right personal qualities are important.

- A number of courses can offer you a broad-based introduction to the leisure industry, including the GCSE in leisure and tourism, AS/A level in leisure studies and various OCR National and BTEC courses. Also, from 2010, Diplomas in sport and leisure are being introduced.

Find out more

Institute for Sport, Parks and Leisure
Abbey Business Centre, 1650 Arlington Business Park, Theale, Reading, Berkshire RG7 4SA.
Tel: 0844 418 0077. www.ispal.org.uk

Institute of Sport and Recreation Management
Sir John Beckwith Centre for Sport, Loughborough University, Loughborough LE11 3TU.
Tel: 01509 226474. www.isrm.co.uk

Sport & Fitness Uncovered – published by Trotman, £11.99.

How to Get Ahead in Leisure & Tourism – published by Heinemann, £12.99.

Working in Cultural Heritage – published by VT Lifeskills, £8.50. Includes profiles of people working in museums and art galleries.

Library and information science and management

Professional librarians and **information managers** are responsible for selecting, buying, storing, organising and using all kinds of materials and media which record information. They work in public libraries, schools, universities, colleges, industry and commerce, the media, national libraries and museums – in fact for any organisation that has information needs.

Looking after information held electronically – on CD-ROMs, DVDs etc – forms an important part of their work.

Information scientists collect and organise information for specific purposes. They are involved in the whole process of information handling, including abstracting, report writing, literature searches and information retrieval. The emphasis of their work is often scientific or technical.

Getting started

- You can start by taking a degree in librarianship, information studies, information management or information science accredited by the Chartered Institute of Library and Information Professionals (CILIP).

- Alternatively, you can do a degree in any other subject (although science, social science or economics are particularly relevant for information science), and then take a specialist postgraduate qualification accredited by the CILIP.

- Once you have completed an accredited course and undertaken a period of professional experience, you can gain chartered membership of the CILIP.

Library and information assistants

Library and information assistants support library and information managers by carrying out the more routine work. Many assistants are not qualified when starting their careers but can study for qualifications while in post.

Getting started

- Five GCSEs at grades A*-C or their equivalent, including English and maths or a science, are often required for entry.

- Once employed, you may study towards City & Guilds qualifications. NVQs are also available.

- You may be able to train through an Apprenticeship.

Find out more

Chartered Institute of Library and Information Professionals
7 Ridgmount Street, London WC1E 7AE.
Tel: 020 7255 0500. www.cilip.org.uk

Aslib, The Association for Information Management
Holywell Centre, 1 Phipp Street, London EC2A 4PS.
Tel: 020 7613 3031. www.aslib.com

Working in English – published by VT Lifeskills, £8.50. Includes a profile of a library assistant.

Licensed conveyancing: see Legal work

Lighting: see Building services engineering

Local government administration

Local authorities run a wide range of public services, including children's services, museums, libraries, social services, refuse collection, street cleaning, parks, and sports and leisure centres. Staff are recruited at all levels, for:

- front-line jobs, such as **reception work, driving** or **manual and craft work** (although often this kind of work is contracted out to private firms)

- **clerical and secretarial** work

- **administration** and **management** positions – available in a wide range of departments

- **specialist posts** needing relevant professional qualifications including accountancy, social work, planning, and environmental health (dealt with elsewhere in this book under the appropriate career).

Getting started

- Graduates of any discipline may be recruited, although degrees such as public administration are particularly appropriate for some jobs. Graduate recruits may follow the National Graduate Development Programme, aimed at those who are capable of becoming senior managers within 10-15 years.

- Applicants with A levels or equivalent qualifications (or even HNDs/foundation degrees) are recruited into general administration, which can lead to management-level work.

- For entry to clerical and secretarial positions, employers may ask for four or perhaps five GCSEs at grades A*-C, to include English and possibly maths, or the equivalent. A GCSE or A level in business studies or applied business could be useful.

- Entry to many areas of work are available through an Apprenticeship.

- Once employed, there are opportunities for promotion and gaining further qualifications through part-time study.

Find out more

Local Government Careers at I&DeA (Improvement and Development Agency)
Layden House, 76-86 Turnmill Street, London EC1M 5LG.
Tel: 020 7296 6880. www.idea.gov.uk and www.LGcareers.com

Working in the Environment (includes profiles of people working in a number of local government jobs) and *Working in Retail & Customer Services* (includes profiles of a local government customer services officer and a trading standards officer) – both published by VT Lifeskills, £8.50 each.

Logistics and transport

The logistics and transport industry is concerned with the delivery of goods and supplies by road, air, rail and sea. The movement of goods – from the factory where they are made through to the customer – is called logistics. Making it all work efficiently calls for people who are flexible and good problem-solvers.

- **Transport/logistics managers** may work for small haulage companies serving local areas through to large organisations responsible for the movement of goods worldwide. Managers have to plan, schedule and look after fleet safety and deal with all other general management duties.

- **Freight forwarders, shipbrokers** and **airbrokers** organise the movement of cargo between countries.

- People are employed at all levels in **distribution and warehouse work** – from lift-truck driving to managing a large distribution centre, such as a warehouse for a major supermarket chain.

● **Drivers** are needed take the goods to their destinations.

Getting started

● **Management-level staff** may work their way up from administrative or supervisory positions, having gained experience and studied part-time for suitable qualifications. Large companies recruit graduates directly into management training. There are degrees in subjects like transport management, but you can enter with any degree subject.

● Apprenticeships and Advanced Apprenticeships are available in road transport operations and distribution and warehousing operations.

● **Drivers** of large lorries/trucks need an LGV licence, which can be taken from the age of 21. However, through the Young LGV Driver Training Scheme, you can gain an LGV licence at a younger age.

Find out more

The Chartered Institute of Logistics and Transport
Earlstrees Court, Earlstrees Road, Corby NN17 4AX.
Tel: 01536 740166. www.ciltuk.org.uk
Publishes a careers information booklet, *Life in the Fast Lane – Career Opportunities in Supply-Chain Management* – can be viewed on the website.

Skills for Logistics
14 Warren Yard, Warren Farm Office Village, Milton Keynes MK12 5NW.
Tel: 01908 313360. www.skillsforlogistics.org

The Institute of Chartered Shipbrokers
85 Gracechurch Street, London EC3V 0AA.
Tel: 020 7623 1111. www.ics.org.uk

Working in Transport & Logistics – published by VT Lifeskills, £8.50.

Distribution and Logistics – from the *Real Life Guides* series – published by Trotman, £9.99.

Management

We may all think we know what managers do – give orders to the rest of us! But there's much more to it than that. Managers are responsible for the effective and efficient running of their team, section or department, or perhaps of the whole organisation. They set aims and targets, carry out long-term planning, deal with the finances – making sure profits are made, budgets kept to, records are maintained etc – and take responsibility for staffing, training, quality control, health and safety and the many other aspects of running a business.

Managers may specialise in a particular area, such as finance, human resources (personnel), purchasing and quality assurance, or they may work as general managers, looking after all aspects of the running of their particular department/office etc.

Managers may also be involved with organisation and methods/work study. This is concerned with measuring and improving efficiency in the workplace – in offices as well as factories.

Getting started

- If you want to aim at management-level work in the future, it may be useful to take a business qualification, such as a GCSE in business studies or applied business, an AS/A level in business studies or applied business or an appropriate OCR National or BTEC qualification. From 2009, Diplomas in business, administration and finance are being introduced.

- It's possible to gradually work your way up into management from a junior level, by gaining experience and studying part time for suitable qualifications.

- Many employers run management training schemes. At least A level (or equivalent) qualifications are required for entry, and often higher-level qualifications, such as a foundation degree, HND or degree, are needed.

- Your degree could be in any subject, but business-based subjects are obviously relevant.

- If you want to specialise in a particular branch of management, such as marketing or human resources, you need to gain the professional qualifications relevant to that field. See entries elsewhere in this book for information on specialist fields.

Find out more

Chartered Management Institute
Management House, Cottingham Road, Corby, Northamptonshire NN17 1TT.
Tel: 01536 204222. www.managers.org.uk

Institute of Administrative Management
6 Graphite Square, Vauxhall Walk, London SE11 5EE.
Tel: 020 7091 2600. www.instam.org

Institute of Management Services
Brooke House, 24 Dam Street, Lichfield WS13 6AB.
Tel: 01543 266909. www.ims-productivity.com
For details on organisation and methods/work study

Marine engineering: see Engineering, Merchant Navy, Royal Navy and Royal Marines

Marines: see Royal Navy and Royal Marines

Market research

Market researchers want to know the demand that exists for their company's products and services, how their products compare with competitors', how different types of advertising and packaging affect sales and so on. There are many ways of collecting this information: the best known is by interviewing the public – over the telephone, or in person. This is done by **interviewers**, often employed on a part-time basis.

Market research executives guide research projects through their various stages, designing questionnaires, and analysing and reporting the findings. **Research assistants** support the executives, by undertaking some of the more routine work.

Getting started

- **Research executive** posts usually require a foundation degree, HND or degree in any subject.

- **Market research assistants** usually need some GCSEs at grades A*-C, including maths and English. A levels, or equivalent qualifications, would be an advantage.

- **Interviewers** do not need formal qualifications, but must enjoy meeting people and be reliable, thorough and methodical.

Find out more

Market Research Society (MRS)
15 Northburgh Street, London EC1V 0JR.
Tel: 020 7490 4911. www.mrs.org.uk

Working in Marketing, Advertising & PR – published by VT Lifeskills, £8.50. Includes a profile of a market research executive.

Marketing

Marketing managers or executives find out what potential customers wish to buy, to make sure that their organisation is providing the products or services that their customers want, at the right price. The work of marketing staff includes the research and testing of possible new products, planning marketing campaigns and dealing with promotion of their products or services. Marketing departments are found in all sorts of organisations – from companies producing the consumer goods that we all buy, through to banks and even colleges!

Marketing managers and executives may be supported in their work by **marketing assistants**.

Getting started

- There is no set entry route. Most entrants aiming at management or executive-level positions hold higher education qualifications. There are degrees in marketing, but graduates of any subject may enter. You can then gain relevant professional qualifications of The Chartered Institute of Marketing (CIM) through part-time study or distance learning.

- Those entering employment may also work towards qualifications of the Institute. The Introductory Certificate provides a basic knowledge of marketing and is available for those with GCSEs at grades A*-C, or equivalent. The Professional Certificate is open to those who have some experience of marketing, or a qualification approved by the CIM (e.g. A levels, an appropriate NVQ level 2 or the Introductory Certificate).

Find out more

The Chartered Institute of Marketing (CIM)
Moor Hall, Cookham, Maidenhead SL6 9QH.
Tel: 01628 427500. www.cim.co.uk

Working in Marketing, Advertising & PR – published by VT Lifeskills, £8.50.

Materials science and metallurgy

Materials scientists apply the science of physics and chemistry to all materials – metal and non-metals. They work both in the production of the material, and its processing into finished products. **Metallurgists** are concerned with the extraction of metals from their ores, and the composition and uses of metals and alloys. Other materials scientists work with non-metallic materials, particularly polymers, ceramics and glass.

Technicians in materials science carry out routine testing and experiments, or may work in quality assurance in the production process.

Getting started

- **Materials science technicians** generally need three or four GCSEs at grades A*-C for entry, or equivalent qualifications. Once employed, training usually includes part-time study for appropriate BTEC National qualifications, which can lead to higher education qualifications.

- Professional-level **metallurgists** and **materials scientists** are graduates. You could take a specialist degree in metallurgy or materials science. Alternatively, you could follow a broader-based degree course in science or engineering and then find a job, or take a relevant postgraduate course first. Maths and a science at A level, or equivalent qualifications, will be needed for entry to a degree course, plus supporting GCSEs. Some degree courses are accredited by The Institute of Materials, Minerals and Mining, and can lead to chartered status.

Find out more

The Institute of Materials, Minerals and Mining
Danum House, South Parade, Doncaster DN 1 2DY.
Tel: 01302 320486. www.iom3.org and www.materials-careers.org.uk

Working in Science – published by VT Lifeskills, £8.50. Includes a profile of a materials engineer.

Mechanical engineering: see Engineering

Mechatronics: see Engineering

Media: radio, TV, film and video/DVD

Commitment and enthusiasm are very important as jobs in the media are extremely competitive to enter.

People with relevant experience – such as in journalism, the arts or theatre – are normally recruited into **production work**. There are opportunities at all levels – from producers, directors and floor managers through to research assistants and runners. Although specific qualifications are not usually requested, most applicants are graduates and have evidence of a strong interest in the media. Degree subject choice can be as wide as the topics that fill radio and TV programmes! Increasingly jobs are advertised on a short-term contract basis (three months to a year – or just to make one programme). Many programmes are made by small, independent companies.

Technical operators include camera operators, sound recordists, lighting specialists and film editors. Many jobs are now done by people who are multiskilled – that is they can operate more than one type of equipment, perhaps sound and camera.

Engineers service and repair the technical equipment.

Presenters may be newsreaders and hosts (interviewing guests, asking questions on quiz shows etc). There are also opportunities for continuity announcers, for people to introduce programme features and for DJs. Presenters may be actors, journalists, celebrities or experts on particular subjects.

Getting started

- If you are interested in a career in media, Diplomas in creative and media may be available.

- Many other courses are available at further education and specialist colleges, many leading to NVQs.

- Whichever media career interests you, try and get experience to prove how keen you are. For example, write for the school magazine if you want to be a broadcast journalist, practise photography, direct your own films, or volunteer for your local hospital radio station.

- The BBC offers a very limited number of training opportunities in production and journalism. Details are on their website. Entry requirements vary, but English and maths GCSE at grades A*-C are likely to be required, with a science or technology subject for technical training. Communication and ICT skills are important. Many applicants have advanced-level or higher education qualifications.

- There are foundation degree, HND and degree courses which specialise in film, video and multi-media production. Some are art and design courses; see *Art and design* for entry requirements. There are also more technical degree courses, with titles like broadcast, digital or media technology.

- Engineers usually have qualifications in electrical engineering, electronics or in communications technology. They enter either as trainee engineers or with a higher education qualification in engineering. See *Engineering* for more details.

Find out more

British Film Institute
21 Stephen Street, London W1T 1LN.
Tel: 020 7255 1444. www.bfi.org.uk

Skillset
Focus Point, 21 Caledonian Road, London N1 9GB.
Tel: 020 7713 9800. Media careers helpline: 08080 300 900.
www.skillset.org
The careers section of Skillset's website contains an A-Z of jobs in film and broadcasting.

BBC Recruitment
PO Box 48305, London W12 6YE.
Tel: 0870 333 1330. www.bbc.co.uk/jobs

FT2
3rd Floor, 18-20 Southwark Street, London SE1 1TJ.
Tel: 020 7407 0344. www.ft2.org.uk

For information about their technical training programmes, see website.

Working in Creative & Media – published by VT Lifeskills, £8.50.

Media Uncovered – published by Trotman, £11.99.

Medical administration work

- **Medical secretaries** work alongside doctors in hospitals and within community health departments. The duties vary from one job to another, but generally medical secretaries' duties include wordprocessing medical reports and letters, keeping records, making appointments for patients and so on.

- **Medical records staff** look after patient records in hospitals and health centres. They also collect information from the records which is used to manage the National Health Service both locally and nationally.

- **Medical receptionists** work in doctors' surgeries and hospitals, making appointments and dealing with patients' queries. Personal qualities, such as being tactful and the ability to deal with people – in particular those who are anxious or upset – are important.

- **Practice managers** are employed by GPs in group practices to manage all aspects of the 'business'.

Getting started

- You can enter **medical secretarial work** with general secretarial/administrative qualifications, and study for specialist qualifications part time whilst in the job, or take a full-time medical secretarial course and then find a job. Four GCSEs at grades A*-C, or equivalent, may be required for entry to college courses.

- There are no formal entry requirements for entry as a **medical records clerk** or **medical receptionist**. Some colleges offer full-time medical reception courses, otherwise you can study part time for relevant qualifications offered by the professional bodies once in the job.

- With A level or equivalent qualifications and a relevant background, **practice managers** (or potential managers) can take the AMSPAR Diploma in Primary Care Management.

Find out more

Association of Medical Secretaries, Practice Managers, Administrators and Receptionists (AMSPAR)
Tavistock House North, Tavistock Square, London WC1H 9LN.
Tel: 020 7387 6005. www.amspar.com

The Institute of Health Record Information and Management
141 Leander Drive, Rochdale OL11 2XE.
Tel: 01706 868481. www.ihrim.co.uk

Working in Hospitals (includes a profile of a medical records clerk) and *Working in Community Healthcare* (includes a profile of a medical receptionist) – both published by VT Lifeskills, £8.50 each.

Medical technology

People working in medical technology operate, monitor and maintain the equipment and machinery used in the diagnosis and treatment of disease. Most of the jobs involve patient contact. In hospitals, such staff may be called medical technical officers. The two main areas of work are medical physics and clinical physiology.

Technicians/technologists in **medical physics** may work in areas such as:

- radiotherapy – used in the treatment of cancer

- ultrasound – producing images e.g. of unborn babies

- nuclear medicine – where scanners are used to detect the uptake of radioactive material which has been introduced into the patient's body

- renal dialysis – monitoring the machines that substitute for kidneys.

While many jobs involve patient contact, others are concerned with routine testing and maintenance.

People who work in **clinical physiology** use equipment to measure how well various parts of the body are working. They may specialise in:

- audiology – testing patients' hearing and balance

- cardiology – measuring heart activity

- neurophysiology – investigating the electrical activity of the brain

- respiratory physiology – checking the efficiency of patients' lungs.

Getting started

- Trainee posts for some areas of work require a minimum of four GCSEs at grades A*-C, including English, maths and two sciences, or equivalent qualifications. Trainees study part time for BTEC National qualifications or for an NVQ, and usually continue their studies to a higher level. In practice, the stiff competition means that jobs often go to applicants with higher-level qualifications.

- Some areas of work, including neurophysiology, require science A levels, or the equivalent, for entry, and trainees study for a degree. For entry to audiology, training is mainly now through a degree, for which an NHS bursary is available, and no fees are payable by the student.

- You have to be 18 for entry to many of the jobs, although in some areas Advanced Apprenticeships and cadetships are available, providing an entry point for various healthcare jobs.

Find out more

NHS Careers
Tel: 0845 60 60 655. www.nhscareers.nhs.uk and www.stepintothenhs.nhs.uk
Produces a range of careers leaflets.

National Leadership and Innovation Agency for Healthcare
For information on training in Wales, click on 'Careers' on: www.nliah.wales.nhs.uk

Institute of Physics and Engineering in Medicine
Fairmount House, 230 Tadcaster Road, York YO24 1ES.
Tel: 01904 610821. www.ipem.org.uk

Working in Hospitals – published by VT Lifeskills, £8.50. Includes a profile of a clinical physiologist.

Medicine and surgery

Doctors diagnose and treat physical and mental health problems. They can work as general practitioners (GPs) running surgeries and visiting patients in their own homes, or in hospitals where they specialise in a medical field such as paediatrics (child health), geriatrics (medical care of older people), psychiatry (mental health) or surgery (operations). A few doctors work in community health where the emphasis is on preventing disease, or in industry and commerce. As well as being interested in science and disease, doctors need excellent communication skills and to be interested in patients as people.

Getting started

- You have to complete a medical degree, taking at least five years, which involves both academic study and patient contact.

- For entry to a medical degree course, three A levels at very high grades are needed, supported by very good grades at GCSE. Chemistry A level is almost always required, plus one of physics, biology or maths (some stipulate biology as the second science). You should check individual prospectuses carefully before choosing subjects at advanced level. Certain qualifications equivalent to A levels may be acceptable.

- After gaining your degree, you undertake a two-year Foundation Programme which provides a bridge between medical school and general practice/specialist training. The Programme involves spending time in a series of placements in a range of specialities and settings.

- Structured, specialist training only begins after the Foundation Programme.

Find out more

British Medical Association
BMA House, Tavistock Square, London WC1H 9JP.
Tel: 020 7387 4499. www.bma.org.uk
Becoming a Doctor is available on the website.

Working in Hospitals and *Working in Community Healthcare* – both published by VT Lifeskills, £8.50 each.

The Essential Guide to Becoming a Doctor – published by Blackwell Publishing.

Medicine Uncovered – published by Trotman, £12.99.

Merchant Navy

Ships of the Merchant Navy transport goods and people. The British fleet consists of ships operated by about 600 shipping companies, working around the UK coastline and worldwide. For this kind of work, you need to be happy working closely with people for long periods, and must be prepared to be away from home for up to several months at a time.

Ratings are able seamen who work under the direction of officers in a range of roles. Shipping companies often recruit ratings from overseas. **Deck/navigating officers** navigate the ship and are responsible for loading and unloading the cargo. They also deal with the commercial management of the ship. **Engineering officers** operate and maintain the ship's engines and other machinery, such as the power generating and cargo handling systems.

Getting started

- All entrants must be fit, able to swim, be in good health, meet the eyesight requirements and have normal colour vision.

- For entry as a **rating**, you should contact shipping companies to enquire about opportunities. Each company sets its own age and entry requirements; employers usually look for some GCSEs. Once employed, ratings work towards NVQs and other qualifications.

- The main route into **officer training** is through a foundation degree (or equivalent qualification) in marine operations (for deck officers) or marine engineering (for engineering officers). Entry requires at least 120 UCAS Tariff points, plus four GCSEs at grades A*-C, including maths, English and science and an additional science or physics.

- You undertake training combining experience at sea with study at nautical college. Along with the foundation degree, you also achieve the professional seafaring Officer of the Watch Certificate of Competency.

- Alternatively, you can be sponsored through a relevant four-year degree course (a year is spent at sea) by a shipping company. For entry to the degree course, you will need at least two A levels, including physics and/or maths, or equivalent, plus supporting GCSEs at grades.

- There are also opportunities for science graduates to enter accelerated officer training.

- School-leavers may be able to enter as officer cadets without the necessary UCAS Tariff points. You will normally need at least four GCSEs at grades A*-C, including maths, English and science and an additional science or physics. You would take a relevant NVQ and HND instead of the foundation degree.

Find out more

Careers at Sea

Carthusian Court, 12 Carthusian Street, London ECIM 6EZ.
Tel: 0800 085 0973 (careers hotline). www.careersatsea.org and www.british-shipping.org

The Marine Society and Sea Cadets

202 Lambeth Road, London SE1 7JW.
Tel: 020 7654 7000. www.ms-sc.org

Working in Transport & Logistics – published by VT Lifeskills, £8.50. Includes a profile of a Merchant Navy deck officer.

Metallurgy: see Materials science and metallurgy

Meteorology

Meteorologists provide weather information, not only for the public through the weather forecasts broadcast on TV and radio, but for others who need to know for work purposes – airlines, shipping companies, farmers. Meteorologists collect data from weather stations, satellites and so on, which they analyse and interpret, using computers. Meteorologists also carry out research on climate change and on improving forecasting methods. The main employer is the Met Office, which is a government agency.

Getting started

- To work as a professional meteorologist, a degree in maths, physics, meteorology or a related subject is required. Degree courses normally require a good base of GCSEs at grades A*-C and at least two A levels in maths and physics, or the equivalent, for entry. Most successful applicants have qualifications above the minimum.

Find out more

Met Office
Fitzroy Road, Exeter, Devon EX1 3PB.
Tel: 0870 900 0100. www.metoffice.gov.uk

Royal Meteorological Society
104 Oxford Road, Reading RG1 7LL.
Tel: 0118 956 8500. www.rmets.org

Midwifery

A midwife is trained to take responsibility for the care of women and their babies in normal childbearing. This includes advising and giving check-ups to expectant mothers, care in labour and responsibility for delivery of the baby. Midwives work in hospitals and in the community, often taking a lead during childbirth.

The midwife continues care of the mother and newborn baby for not less than 10 days and sometimes up to the 28th day. Where an abnormality arises in a mother or baby, the midwife is trained to assess this and refer the mother and/or the baby to a medical practitioner.

Getting started

- Entry is through a full-time degree course, usually lasting three years. At least two A levels, preferably including a science subject, are required for entry, plus supporting GCSEs at grades A*-C, to include English, maths and science.

- It is possible for qualified nurses to train as a midwife through an 18-month, full-time course.

Find out more

NHS Careers
Tel: 0845 60 60 655. www.nhscareers.nhs.uk and www.stepintothenhs.nhs.uk
Produces a range of careers leaflets.

National Leadership and Innovation Agency for Healthcare
For information on training in Wales, click on 'Careers' on: www.nliah.wales.nhs.uk

See also website of the **Royal College of Midwives**: www.rcm.org.uk

Nursing & Midwifery Uncovered – published by Trotman, £11.99.

Mining and minerals engineering: see
Engineering

Motor vehicle work

Vehicle engineers design and develop new vehicles, and are responsible for the manufacturing process. Professional engineers are assisted by technicians, who help with testing, quality control and so on.

Motor vehicle technicians service and repair motor vehicles, which increasingly involves the use of electronic diagnostic equipment. Some specialise in heavy vehicles (trucks/buses etc) or in motorcycles. There is currently a shortage of skilled technicians.

Fast-fit staff work in specialist workshops replacing car, van and motorbike tyres, exhausts or batteries, usually while the customer waits.

Getting started

- For professional **vehicle engineering** design and manufacturing, you will need an accredited engineering degree.

- Entry to **motor vehicle technician** work usually requires at least four GCSEs at grades A*-C, including maths, English and science, or equivalent. Training is normally through an Apprenticeship. There are also some full-time college courses to get you started. Entry requirements vary.

- You do not usually need academic qualifications for entry to **fast-fit work**. Training will be provided by your employer, possibly leading to NVQs. It may be possible to train through an Apprenticeship.

- Some 14- to 16-year-olds may have the opportunity to take a Young Apprenticeship in the motor industry, combining learning and work experience with an employer with study at school and college.

- If you are interested in motor vehicle work, Diplomas in engineering may be available and Diplomas in manufacturing and product design are being introduced from 2009.

Find out more

Automotive Skills
Fanshaws, Brickendon, Hertford SG13 7DP.
Tel: 01992 511521. www.automotiveskills.org.uk

The Institute of the Motor Industry
Fanshaws, Brickendon, Hertford SG13 8PQ.
Tel: 01992 511521. www.motor.org.uk

A website also giving information on education, training and careers: www.autoindustry.co.uk

The Motor Industry – from the *Real Life Guides* series – published by Trotman, £9.99.

Multimedia/interactive media: see
Information and communication technology

Museum work

Curators are responsible for the organisation of a museum, or a particular museum department. They acquire, catalogue and display the exhibits. They may run museum clubs for children and liaise with schools, or specialist **educational staff** may be employed to do this. Some curators are allowed time to do their own research work. **Conservation officers** monitor the condition of exhibits, and carry out necessary treatment. **Museum assistants/attendants** and **visitor services staff** assist with the day-to-day running of the museum. There is a lot of competition for jobs.

Getting started

- **Curators** need a degree in a relevant subject, such as archaeology, anthropology, history or science, according to the kind of collection. A postgraduate qualification is usually necessary.

- For **conservation work**, you will need to take a relevant degree and postgraduate course.

- Apprenticeships are available as an entry route into assistant/ support-level work.

Find out more

Museums Association
24 Calvin Street, London E1 6NW.
Tel: 020 7426 6910. www.museumsassociation.org
Working in Cultural Heritage – published by VT Lifeskills, £8.50.

Music

Professional musicians work as **composers, performers** – playing instruments, singing and conducting – and **teachers**. Performers may work in large orchestras, in small groups or solo. This is a highly competitive career. Classical musicians have virtually all followed a formal training, whilst pop, folk and jazz musicians have rarely followed formal training.

Getting started

- There are specialist music colleges offering degree courses with the emphasis on **performance**. Degrees in music are also available at universities and colleges of higher education. These vary widely – there are courses specialising in popular music, jazz studies, electronic music and so on, as well as classical music. For entry to performance-based music degree courses, in addition to the academic entry requirements, you will need a very high standard of musical ability.

- Those who wish to be class **teachers** in state schools need to gain a degree leading to Qualified Teacher Status, or a degree in music followed by a postgraduate certificate in education. You will need GCSEs at grades A*-C in English and maths, and, for primary school teaching, in science.

- BTEC National courses in popular music are run at many colleges. These often need four GCSEs at grades A*-C for entry.

- GCSEs, AS/A levels and other qualifications are available in the performing arts.

Find out more

Incorporated Society of Musicians
10 Stratford Place, London W1C 1AA.
Tel: 020 7629 4413. www.ism.org

See the Society's website for *Careers with Music* and information sheets – *The First 10 Years: Establishing a Solo Career* and *The First 2 Years: Establishing an Orchestral Career.*

British Phonographic Society
Music Education Department, Riverside Building, County Hall, Westminster Bridge Road, London SE1 7JA.
Tel: 020 7803 1300. www.bpi.co.uk
Produces the *Music Education Directory.*

Access to Music
Lionel House, 35 Millstone Lane, Leicester LE1 5JN.
Course information line: 0800 281842. www.accesstomusic.co.uk
Offers a range of training courses for those wanting to get into the pop music industry.

Working in Music – published by VT Lifeskills, £8.50.

Music Industry Uncovered – published by Trotman, £11.99.

Working in the Music Industry – published by How To Books, £9.99.

Music therapy: see Creative therapies

Nanny work: see Early years childcare and education

Nature conservation: see Environmental work

Naturopathy: see Complementary medicine

Naval architecture: see Engineering

Navy: see Royal Navy and Royal Marines

Nursery nursing: see Early years childcare and education

Nursing

As well as caring for adult patients and children in hospitals, **nurses** care for people with learning disabilities and those with mental health problems. Once qualified, there are other jobs that nurses move into within the community, such as **district nurse** – visiting people at home, or **health visitor** – working with families with young children or with older people. Nurses also work in GPs' practices, in schools and in industry.

You train for one of four branches – adult, children's nursing, learning disability nursing or mental health nursing. Nurses can progress to senior positions, such as nurse consultant.

Getting started

- To qualify as a registered nurse, you need to take either a three-year nursing diploma or degree course.

- Training institutions generally look for around five GCSEs at grades A*-C for entry to the diploma course (GCSE English, maths and a science may be specified) or an approved alternative qualification. However, many successful applicants hold higher qualifications.

- Degree course entry is also competitive – while the minimum entry requirement is two A levels, some institutions ask for three A levels (or equivalent qualifications) plus supporting GCSEs. Each course sets its own particular entry requirements, which may be higher. A science at A level may be required, together with specific GCSE subjects at grades A*-C.

- There are a number of different types of courses in health and social care – from GCSEs to BTEC National and OCR National qualifications. In addition, Diplomas in society, health and development may be available. All these courses can provide a broad introduction, but check their acceptability for nurse training.

- Financial help is available for trainee nurses. Degree students on NHS-funded places have their tuition fees paid and can apply for means-tested bursaries to help towards living expenses. Financial arrangements differ in Wales, Scotland and Northern Ireland.

N.B Nursing diplomas are not available in Wales, where training is through a degree.

Find out more

NHS Careers
Tel: 0845 60 60 655. www.nhscareers.nhs.uk and
www.stepintothenhs.nhs.uk
Produces a range of careers leaflets.

National Leadership and Innovation Agency for Healthcare
For information on training in Wales, click on 'Careers' on:
www.nliah.wales.nhs.uk

Working in Hospitals and *Working in Community Healthcare* – both published by VT Lifeskills, £8.50 each.

Nursing & Midwifery Uncovered – published by Trotman, £11.99.

For current details of NHS bursaries for nurse training, view:
www.nhsstudentgrants.co.uk

Occupational therapy

Occupational therapists (OTs) help people who have physical, social and/or psychological problems to be as independent as possible in their everyday lives. OTs identify what is preventing their clients from carrying out everyday activities – such as cooking or moving around – and work out ways of coping with or overcoming such problems.

OT assistants (also called OT support workers) assist professional OTs in their work.

Getting started

- To qualify as an **OT**, most people complete a degree course approved by the Health Professions Council (HPC). For entry, you need at least two A levels (in practice, three are often needed) or equivalent qualifications, plus supporting GCSEs at grades A*-C. The subjects required vary between the courses, but at A level, at least one science or social science subject may be required or preferred, together with maths, science and English at GCSE.

- Alternatively, there are HPC-approved two-year, full-time courses for those with a relevant first degree.

- Those who are already employed as OT assistants may train through an in-service training course, leading to a degree.

- You do not necessarily need any academic qualifications to get started as an **OT assistant** – although individual employers may set their own entry requirements. Having the right personal qualities is very important.

Find out more

British Association/College of Occupational Therapists
106-114 Borough High Street, Southwark, London SE1 1LB.
Tel: 020 7357 6480. www.cot.co.uk
Publishes the annual *Careers Handbook*, which lists degree programmes (can be downloaded from the website).

NHS Careers
Tel: 0845 60 60 655. www.nhscareers.nhs.uk and www.stepintothenhs.nhs.uk
Produces a range of careers leaflets.

National Leadership and Innovation Agency for Healthcare
For information on training in Wales, click on 'Careers' on: www.nliah.wales.nhs.uk

Health Professions Council
Park House, 184 Kennington Park Road, London SE11 4BU.
Tel: 020 7582 0866. www.hpc-uk.org
Website gives details of standards and approved courses.

Working in Community Healthcare – published by VT Lifeskills, £8.50.
Includes a profile of an occupational therapist.

Oceanography

Oceanography is the scientific study of the oceans. It combines many different scientific disciplines, such as marine biology, marine geology, marine chemistry and physical oceanography. People specialising in these areas work together to find out more about the world's oceans, and research into problems such as pollution, how to conserve fish stocks and climate change.

Getting started

- You need a degree, and most entrants also hold postgraduate qualifications. Your degree could be in any science subject, followed by a specialist postgraduate qualification in oceanography.

- Alternatively, there are some first degrees that cover oceanography or ocean sciences, usually in combination with another subject. Entry requirements vary according to the subject, so you will need to check with individual courses, but science A level subjects are generally needed (or the equivalent), and possibly maths, together with supporting GCSEs at grades A*-C.

Find out more

Institute of Marine Engineering, Science and Technology
80 Coleman Street, London EC2R 5BJ.
Tel: 020 7382 2600. www.imarest.org
Sea Your Future can be viewed on the website.

Society of Underwater Technology
Address as above.
Tel: 020 7382 2601. www.sut.org

National Oceanography Centre, Southampton
University of Southampton, Waterfront Campus, European Way, Southampton SO14 3ZH.
Tel: 023 8059 6666. www.noc.soton.ac.uk

Operating department practice

Operating department practitioners (ODPs) work in hospital operating theatres undertaking some of the more routine work before, during and after operations. Their duties include checking that the patient is the right person for the operation, that the correct records, X-rays etc are available, preparing and handing instruments and equipment to the surgeon during the operation, checking the patient's recovery afterwards (with other team members), and cleaning all equipment.

ODPs need to be very methodical, calm under pressure and prepared to work shifts, including at nights and weekends.

N.B. Don't confuse this job with that of **operating department orderlies** who do all the unskilled lifting, carrying and cleaning jobs in the operating theatre.

Getting started

- By law, to work as an ODP, you must be registered with the Health Professions Council (HPC) having completed an HPC-approved course.

- Training is a mixture of practical work at hospital and study at university for a Diploma of Higher Education.

- There are no set entry requirements – individual training centres set their own – but you are likely to need five GCSEs at grades A*-C including English, maths and science. Some courses also require A levels, or equivalent qualifications.

Find out more

NHS Careers
Tel: 0845 60 60 655. www.nhscareers.nhs.uk and
www.stepintothenhs.nhs.uk
Produces a range of careers leaflets.

National Leadership and Innovation Agency for Healthcare
For information on training in Wales, click on 'Careers' on:
www.nliah.wales.nhs.uk

Health Professions Council
Park House, 184 Kennington Road, London SE11 4BU.
Tel: 020 7582 0866. www.hpc-uk.org
Website gives details of standards and approved courses.

College of Operating Department Practitioners
197-199 City Road, London EC1V 1JN.
Tel: 0870 746 0984. www.codp.org

Working in Hospitals – published by VT Lifeskills, £8.50. Includes a profile of a senior ODP.

Optometry (ophthalmic optics)

Optometrists (also known as ophthalmic opticians) test and examine eyes, and prescribe glasses and contact lenses. They must be able to recognise diseases of the eye, and refer patients on to medical specialists.

Optometrists work in high street practices, in NHS clinics and hospitals.

Getting started

- Entry is through a degree course in optometry, approved by The General Optical Council.

- For entry to a degree course, three A levels (at high grades) are needed – to include at least two from maths, physics, biology and chemistry. Some courses specify certain A level subjects. You will need supporting GCSEs at grades A*-C, including English. Alternative equivalent qualifications may be acceptable, but usually only if offered in addition to A levels.

Find out more

The General Optical Council

41 Harley Street, London W1G 8DJ.
Tel: 020 7580 3898. www.optical.org
A career in vision care can be downloaded from the website.

The College of Optometrists

41-42 Craven Street, London WC2N 5NG.
Tel: 020 7839 6000. www.college-optometrists.org

Working in Community Healthcare – published by VT Lifeskills, £8.50.
Includes a profile of an optometrist.

Orthoptics

Orthoptists work as part of the eye-care team, diagnosing and treating defects of binocular vision such as squints and disorders of eye muscle movements. A lot of the work is with children, in hospitals and health centres, but adult patients are also referred for assessment and treatment.

Getting started

- You need to take an orthoptics degree course, approved by the Health Professions Council, available at Liverpool and Sheffield Universities.

- For entry, three A levels (at high grades) are normally required; Liverpool requires biology and Sheffield prefers it. Equivalent qualifications may be acceptable, at the discretion of the institution. You will need supporting GCSEs at grades A*-C, including English, sciences and maths.

Find out more

British and Irish Orthoptic Society
Tavistock House North, Tavistock Square, London WC1H 9HX.
Tel: 020 7387 7992. www.orthoptics.org.uk

NHS Careers
Tel: 0845 60 60 655. www.nhscareers.nhs.uk and
www.stepintothenhs.nhs.uk
Produces a range of careers leaflets.

National Leadership and Innovation Agency for Healthcare
For information on training in Wales, click on 'Careers' on:
www.nliah.wales.nhs.uk

Health Professions Council
Park House, 184 Kennington Road, London SE11 4BU.
Tel: 020 7582 0866. www.hpc-uk.org
Website gives details of standards and approved courses.

Osteopathy: see Chiropractic and osteopathy

Painting and decorating: see Building crafts

Paralegal work: see Legal work

Paramedical work: see Ambulance service work

Patent work

New inventions are patented with the Intellectual Property Office, in order to protect the idea or invention from being copied for up to 20 years.

Inventors go to **patent agents** (or patent attorneys) to act on their behalf in the patenting process. Patent agents check whether the invention is really original, and present the case to the Intellectual Property Office.

Patent agents work in private practice or in large industrial firms.

Patent examiners work in the Intellectual Property Office and examine applications for patents to ensure that only really new inventions qualify for granted patents.

Trade marks is a related area of work; **trade mark attorneys** provide advice during the development of new trade marks. Attention to detail is particularly important for these areas of work.

Getting started

- To be a **patent agent** you need a degree in science, maths or engineering. Graduates are then employed as technical assistants, and study for the exams of the Chartered Institute of Patent Attorneys. To practise before the European Patent Office, a further examination must be passed.

- To work as a **patent examiner**, you need a degree in science, engineering, maths or an equivalent professional qualification/ experience. On-the-job training is given. Foreign language skills are also important.

Find out more

The Chartered Institute of Patent Attorneys
95 Chancery Lane, London WC2A 1DT.
Tel: 020 7405 9450. www.cipa.org.uk

Intellectual Property Office
Concept House, Cardiff Road, Newport, Gwent NP10 8QQ.
Tel: 01633 814000. www.ipo.gov.uk

Working in Science – published by VT Lifeskills, £8.50. Includes a profile of a patent attorney.

Personal adviser (Connexions): see Careers work, Youth and community work

Personnel work: see Human resource management

Pharmacy

Pharmacists dispense medicines to the public. Most pharmacists work in community pharmacies (retail chemists' shops or health centres), where they supply medicines that have been prescribed by a doctor, and supervise the sale of medicines that may be sold only under the supervision of a pharmacist. They also advise customers on the proper use of medicines and on a variety of healthcare issues. Hospital pharmacists, in addition to dispensing medicines, may advise their medical and nursing colleagues on the effects of medicines. Industrial pharmacists are involved in a wide variety of occupations: research, production, marketing, and in providing technical and medical information.

Pharmacy technicians work under the supervision of a pharmacist, dispensing prescriptions in chemists shops and hospitals.

Getting started

- To be a **pharmacist**, you need to start by taking a pharmacy degree. For entry, three A levels including chemistry and at least one other scientific subject are required (sometimes two), plus at least five GCSEs at grades A*-C, including English and maths. Qualifications equivalent to GCSEs and A levels may be acceptable, but check in prospectuses.

- To practise as a community or hospital pharmacist, you must follow your degree by one year's practical pre-registration training, and must pass the Royal Pharmaceutical Society's registration examination.

- For **pharmacy technician** work, employers usually look for applicants holding four or five GCSEs, including English, maths and a science subject at grade A*-C, or equivalent. Trainees work towards an NVQ level 3 in pharmacy services whilst in employment. You may be able to train through an Advanced Apprenticeship.

It is not possible to start as a pharmacy technician and work your way up to becoming a pharmacist without taking a pharmacy degree course.

Find out more

Royal Pharmaceutical Society of Great Britain
1 Lambeth High Street, London SE1 7JN.
Tel: 020 7572 2330. www.rpsgb.org.uk/education/careersindex.html

The leaflets, *Interested in Pharmacy?* and *Career as a pharmacy technician*, are available to download from the website.

National Pharmacy Association
Mallinson House, 38-42 St Peter's Street, St Albans ALI 3NP.
Tel: 01727 832161. www.npa.co.uk
Working in a pharmacy leaflet can be downloaded from the website.

Working in Community Healthcare (includes a profile of a pharmacist) and *Working in Science* (includes a profile of a pharmacy technician) – both published by VT Lifeskills, £8.50 each.

Photography

Photographs are required for advertising, illustration, portraits and scientific and medical work. Photographers usually specialise in a particular area of photography – such as fashion photography or general practice (taking family portraits, wedding photographs and so on). Whatever the specialism, you need creative and technical skills, the ability to relate to people and great determination, as it is a competitive profession.

Getting started

- While it is possible to start as a junior or an assistant without relevant qualifications, and work your way up through part-time study, this is not an easy way in.

- There is a range of full-time photography courses at colleges and universities, from City & Guilds to degree level. These provide a useful starting point for developing your skills, but cannot guarantee to lead to a job. For entry to courses, as well as the academic requirements, you usually need a portfolio of work as evidence of your interest and ability.

- You may be able to get started through an Apprenticeship or Advanced Apprenticeship in photo imaging.

- For entry to press photography, you can apply to a newspaper for direct entry to a traineeship, which requires at least five GCSEs at grades A*-C, including English, or the equivalent. As there is often a lot of competition for these positions, many applicants have degrees. Alternatively you can take a one-year, pre-entry course, approved by the National Council for the Training of Journalists. These require at least one A level (sometimes two), plus supporting GCSEs for entry.

- If you are interested in a career in photography, Diplomas in creative and media may be available.

Find out more

British Institute of Professional Photography
Fox Talbot House, Amwell End, Ware, Hertfordshire SG12 9HN.
Tel: 01920 464011. www.bipp.com

Association of Photographers
81 Leonard Street, London EC2A 4QS.
Tel: 020 7739 6669. www.the-aop.org
You can download a career pack, written by professional photographers, from the website.

National Council for the Training of Journalists
The New Granary, Station Road, Newport, Saffron Walden, Essex CB11 3PL.
Tel: 01799 544014. www.nctj.com
For information about press photography training.

For information on careers in photography, including profiles of different photographers, and details of courses and qualifications see: www.skillset.org/photo

Working in Creative & Media – published by VT Lifeskills, £8.50. Includes a profile of a photographer.

Physics

Physics is the study of matter and energy. Physicists apply their knowledge in fields like electronics, space science, optics, acoustics and medical physics. They need to be curious about how things work and have good analytical and observational skills. Physicists are employed by a wide range of organisations, from small research laboratories to multi-national companies.

Getting started

- To become a professional physicist, you need a degree and sometimes a postgraduate qualification.

- For a degree in physics or a related subject, you need at least two A levels (in practice most courses require three) or equivalent. Two of your A levels should be in maths and physics. You also need supporting GCSEs at grades A*-C, including science and an additional science (or physics and another separate science) and maths.

Find out more

Institute of Physics
76 Portland Place, London W1B 1NT.
Tel: 020 7470 4800. www.iop.org

Working in Science – published by VT Lifeskills, £8.50.

Careers with a Science Degree – published by Lifetime Publishing, £11.99.

Physiological measurement: see Medical technology

Physiotherapy

Physiotherapists work within a healthcare team and treat people with physical problems resulting from accident, illness or the onset of old age. They may use manual therapy, electrical treatments, water therapy or massage. They also teach patients exercises and some of the work may be preventative. Physiotherapists work in hospitals and in the community. Patience and good communication and observational skills are required.

Physiotherapy assistants (also called clinical support workers) support qualified physiotherapists. The work involves considerable patient contact, e.g. supervising patients doing exercises, motivating patients, assisting with dressing etc.

N.B. Some **sports therapists**, who have qualified as physiotherapists, work with athletes or professional sports teams to help them to train safely or recover from an injury.

Getting started

- Although there are no set entry requirements to work as a **physiotherapy assistant**, you may need at least four GCSEs at grades A*-C, or the equivalent, for more advanced-level work.

- To practise as a **physiotherapist** you have to hold a degree approved by the Health Professions Council. For entry, you need three A levels, or equivalent, including a biological science, and supporting GCSEs at grades A*-C, including English, maths and a spread of sciences.

- You need to be physically fit.

Find out more

Chartered Society of Physiotherapy
14 Bedford Row, London WC1R 4ED.
Tel: 020 7306 6666. www.csp.org.uk

NHS Careers
Tel: 0845 60 60 655. www.nhscareers.nhs.uk and
www.stepintothenhs.nhs.uk
Produces a range of careers leaflets.

National Leadership and Innovation Agency for Healthcare
For information on training in Wales, click on 'Careers' on:
www.nliah.wales.nhs.uk

Health Professions Council
Park House, 184 Kennington Road, London SE11 4BU.
Tel: 020 7582 0866. www.hpc-uk.org
Website gives details of standards and approved courses.

Working in Hospitals (includes a profile of a physiotherapist) and *Working in Community Healthcare* (includes a profile of a sports physiotherapist) – both published by VT Lifeskills, £8.50 each.

Piloting (air)

Commercial pilots fly aircraft on either long-haul or short-haul flights. Before they take off, they ensure that checks are carried out. The captain is in command and is responsible for the safety of the aircraft, the passengers and crew. Most modern commercial aircraft have two pilots, although a second crew may be carried on very long flights. Apart from working for airlines, pilots spray crops, make test flights and aerial surveys, and give flying instruction.

Pilots need physical and mental coordination, the ability to keep calm and excellent communication and teamwork skills.

Getting started

- To get experience of flying, you could take private lessons or join an organisation such as the Air Cadets, The Air League or your University Air Squadron.

- To be a commercial airline or helicopter pilot, you must hold an appropriate licence issued by the Civil Aviation Authority. For all pilot training, you must be medically fit. The course fees and expenses are up to £70,000, so try to gain sponsorship from an airline (the minimum age is 18).

- It's also possible to train as a pilot with the RAF and then undertake further training and testing to become a commercial pilot.

- The usual minimum entry requirements for full-time sponsored training are five GCSEs at grades A*-C, including English, maths and a science, plus two A levels, preferably in maths and physics, or equivalent. However, many pilots have degrees.

Find out more

The British Air Line Pilots' Association
www.balpa.org
The booklet, *How to become a Commercial Pilot*, can be downloaded from the website.

For information about Armed Forces flying training, contact your local **Armed Forces Careers Office**.

Planning

Planners (commonly known as town and country planners) try to shape a better environment. They investigate the options for siting new building developments, recommend whether a planning application should be approved and ensure that building does not go ahead without permission. Planners are employed in a range of organisations, e.g. local government, central government and its agencies, private companies and consultancies. Planners need good decision-making, teamworking and communication skills.

Planning technicians deal with the more routine and practical tasks, e.g. gathering information, dealing with paperwork, producing graphics and illustrations, carrying out surveys, producing reports and analysing data.

Getting started

- To become a **professional planner**, you could take a planning degree course accredited by the RTPI. Useful advanced-level subjects include geography, economics, maths and sciences. Supporting GCSEs, including maths and English, are also normally required. Alternatively, you could take a degree in a related subject, such as geography or architecture, followed by an RTPI-accredited postgraduate course on a full- or part-time basis. Another possible route is to take a distance-learning course. There are no set entry requirements but it can take up to eight years to complete!

- Once you have gained your RTPI-approved qualification in planning, and have completed practical experience, you can apply for chartered status with the RTPI.

- There are no set entry requirements for employment as a **planning technician** although GCSEs at grades A*-C in English, maths and other appropriate subjects, or equivalent, are normally expected. Once in employment, you can work towards an NVQ in built environment development (available at levels 3 and 4) or a relevant foundation degree or Higher National qualification. It is possible to work your way up to become professionally qualified.

Find out more

Royal Town Planning Institute (RTPI)
41 Botolph Lane, London EC3R 8DL.
Tel: 020 7929 9494. www.rtpi.org.uk

Working in the Environment – published by VT Lifeskills, £8.50. Includes profiles of an assistant planning officer and an assistant building control officer.

Plant operating: see Building crafts

Plastering: see Building crafts

Play therapy: see Creative therapies

Playwork

Playworkers help to provide opportunities for children from the age of four to 16 to play in different ways and in different settings. They find ways to stimulate children through play, helping them to build relationships and become independent. They plan and supervise play, organise materials and equipment and keep basic records.

Playworkers are employed by local authorities, private providers and voluntary groups. Work is mainly during out-of-school hours and can be at adventure playgrounds, play centres, out-of-school clubs, holiday playschemes, on play buses and in hospitals.

Getting started

- Most people gain experience through voluntary work before finding paid employment in playwork.

- There is usually an induction programme for new entrants and in-service courses are provided by some employers.

- Training and qualifications are available at all levels. Most employees take a relevant qualification while in employment. CACHE level 2 Certificate and level 3 Diploma courses are available in playwork. For the Diploma, you may need some GCSEs at grades A*-C, or equivalent. NVQs in playwork are available at levels 2-4; these can be achieved through assessment in the workplace.

- It's possible to get started through an Apprenticeship or Advanced Apprenticeship.

- Higher education courses, such as foundation degrees, Higher National qualifications and degrees are available in playwork.

Find out more

SkillsActive
Castlewood House, 77-91 New Oxford Street, London WC1A 1PX.
Tel: 020 7632 2000. www.skillsactive.com and www.playwork.org.uk

Plumbing: see Building crafts

Podiatry

Foot problems affect over half the population, so there is a lot of job satisfaction to be had in easing people's pain and discomfort. **Podiatrists** provide specialist foot care and advice, including performing minor surgery, working within the NHS in hospitals and health clinics or in their own private surgeries. They deal with children's foot problems, sports injuries, foot deformities, foot care for older people and for patients with conditions such as rheumatoid arthritis and diabetes. Podiatrists are supported in their work by **footcare assistants**.

N.B. The terms 'podiatry' and 'podiatrist' are gradually replacing 'chiropody' and 'chiropodist'.

Getting started

- You don't usually need particular formal qualifications to start training as a **footcare assistant**, but you do need good communication skills and to be a caring person.

- To qualify as a **podiatrist**, you have to take a degree course approved by the Health Professions Council. A good base of GCSEs at grades A*-C, plus two A levels – including one science subject – are normally required for entry. Other equivalent qualifications may be acceptable.

Find out more

Society of Chiropodists and Podiatrists
1 Fellmongers Path, Tower Bridge Road, London SE1 3LY.
Tel: 020 7234 8620. www.feetforlife.org

Health Professions Council
Park House, 184 Kennington Road, London SE11 4BU.
Tel: 020 7582 0866. www.hpc-uk.org
Website gives details of standards and approved courses.

Working in Community Healthcare – published by VT Lifeskills, £8.50. Includes a profile of a podiatrist.

Police and security services

Police officers are responsible for maintaining law and order and making sure that the public and their property are protected. They also investigate crimes and are concerned with crime prevention. Police officers need to have good problem-solving skills and the ability to stay calm and in control in difficult situations.

Police community support officers are civilian staff employed to support the public and assist police officers. They have powers to make limited searches and hand out fixed-penalty notices, but they have no powers of arrest.

Security officers work for private security firms guarding premises, and/ or transporting large amounts of cash or valuables from banks and other businesses.

Getting started

- For all police and security jobs you have to be physically fit and in good health.

- The youngest age at which you can become a **police constable** is 18. A few police forces operate volunteer cadet schemes for 14- to 18-year-olds.

- Although no formal educational requirements are set by the police force, you must be able to cope with the training to succeed in the job. You will undertake various tests during the selection process.

- There are further and higher education courses that can help prepare you for entry to the police force, e.g. the BTEC First and BTEC National in public services. Diplomas in public services are being introduced from 2010.

- All new police officers undergo a two-year training period called the Initial Police Learning and Development Programme. During this time you undertake intensive training and spend the rest of the time on the beat. A fast-track High Potential Development Scheme exists for entrants with particular promise regardless of their academic background.

- You don't need any formal qualifications for entry as a **police community support officer**, but you will have to pass various tests.

- Individual security firms set their own entrance requirements, but preference is often given if you have some GCSE passes.

Find out more

To find out more about the different roles within the police force, and entry requirements visit: www.policecouldyou.co.uk

The Police Force – from the *Real Life Guides* series – published by Trotman, £9.99.

Working in Police, Fire & Security – published by VT Lifeskills, £8.50.

Polymer technology: see Materials science and metallurgy

Postal services

The Royal Mail Group is a government-owned organisation comprising the companies described below. There are job opportunities at all levels.

Post Office – this is the retail side of the Royal Mail Group. Customer service advisers sell stamps, handle mail, deal with financial services like National Savings, take bill payments, provide government information, issue certain licences etc.

Royal Mail – advanced machines at large sorting offices handle thousands of letters an hour but some sorting is still done by hand. In local offices, mail is split into rounds for delivery. Job opportunities include postal delivery/collection and administration.

Parcelforce Worldwide – this company is involved in the competitive market of parcel delivery and has a worldwide distribution service. There are opportunities for drivers, sorters, clerical workers etc.

There are also opportunities with private postal delivery companies which are licensed to deliver mail.

Getting started

- For most jobs in the Royal Mail Group you do not require specific qualifications for entry, although GCSEs in English and maths at grades A*-C are always useful.

- You will be given aptitude tests and an interview as part of the selection process.

- Training is provided for all jobs – this may be a combination of on- and off-the-job training. NVQs are available in mail operations and can be gained through assessment in the workplace.

- 18-month Apprenticeships are available – young people are employed and work towards NVQs in mail services.

- Existing employees can gain promotion to supervisory and management-level positions, or you could enter as a graduate through a management training scheme.

Find out more

Contact your nearest Royal Mail delivery office, Post Office or private delivery company for information about job opportunities in your area.

Royal Mail Group plc
www.royalmailgroup.com
Website contains information on careers and vacancies.

Working in Retail & Customer Services – published by VT Lifeskills, £8.50. Includes a profile of a Post Office clerk.

Poultry farming: see Farming and agricultural advisory work

Practice management (GP): see Medical administration work

Printing

Printing firms produce a wide range of material from the obvious books, newspapers and magazines to labels, wallpaper, cardboard boxes and plastic bags. Computers are an integral part of the modern printing process. Some of the jobs include:

- **graphic reproduction** – cameras and electronic scanners are used to incorporate artwork and photographs

- **planning** – arranging the pages in the right position for cutting, folding or trimming

- **platemaking** – transferring the material to the type of printing plate needed for the chosen process

- **machine printing** – preparing and operating different printing presses, most of which are computer controlled – this may involve positioning printing plates in the press, taking trial prints, mixing inks, conducting quality checks and maintaining the press

- **print finishing** – using machines (or hands) to cut, trim, drill, fold, glue or stitch the printed materials.

Printing technologists or **managers** oversee the whole printing process. After discussion with the customer, they choose the most suitable paper and printing medium for the job, estimate the final cost and ensure a smooth workflow.

Getting started

- For most jobs, you need to have normal colour vision, be able to pay attention to detail and have the ability to handle delicate materials, such as film and photographic paper.

- For entry to **craft trades**, you may need GCSEs at grade A*-C in English, maths, science and technology subjects, or equivalent qualifications.

- Training is usually on the job with part-time study. Apprenticeships and Advanced Apprenticeships offer young people training leading to NVQs. There are also full- and part-time college courses in printing, e.g. leading to BTEC National or City & Guilds qualifications.

- For **printing technology/management**, there are printing-related foundation degrees, HNDs and degrees and higher-education courses in business or management which include printing modules or options. Some courses include a sandwich year.

Find out more

British Printing Industries Federation
Training Department, 2 Viller's Court, Meridien Business Park, Copse Drive, Coventry CV5 9RN.
Tel: 01676 526030. www.britishprint.com

Institute of Paper, Printing and Publishing
83 Guildford Street, Chertsey, Surrey KT16 9AS.
Tel: 0870 330 8625. www.ip3.org.uk

Prison work

The Prison Service keeps people who have been sentenced to prison securely in custody. Education, training and counselling are also provided to help prisoners make a fresh start. Different kinds of custody are provided to suit different types and ages of offenders. The HM Prison Service employs **prison officers** and **operational managers** but there are also jobs for **support staff** and for **specialists** such as prison psychologists, teachers and religious workers. Prison staff need patience, control, confidence, a mature attitude and a readiness to treat all prisoners equally.

N.B. Some prisons and young offenders' institutions are built, managed and operated by private companies contracted out by the Home Office. Their employment and training policies will differ from those described here.

Getting started

- For entry as a **prison officer**, you have to be aged 18 or over and be a British, EU or Commonwealth citizen. You also have to be physically fit and in good general health.

- All applicants must pass some aptitude tests and undergo a medical examination, further tests assessing fitness and a selection interview. New prison officers do eight weeks' basic training spent both in a prison and at a training centre.

- All new prison officers must achieve an NVQ level 3 in custodial care within 12 months of starting their position.

- Prison officers are able to achieve promotion to **operational manager** grades. Alternatively, there is a scheme which gives applicants with a degree, or equivalent qualifications, or with managerial experience, a fast route to operational manager status.

Find out more

Recruitment of prison officers is dealt with at local level – contact the manager of your local prison (look in local directories, or a list of prisons is on the website below).

HM Prison Service
Cleland House, Page Street, London SW1P 4LN.
www.hmprisonservice.gov.uk/careersandjobs
See website for information on graduate recruitment and the Intensive Development Scheme for operational managers.

For details of privately-managed prisons, see
www.hmprisons.gov.uk/prisoninformation/privateprison

Probation work and community justice

The main duty of a **probation officer** is to protect members of the public by helping offenders change their ways. They aim to rehabilitate offenders back into society. They may attend court, work with offenders who have received community orders for their crimes and help prisoners and those who have just been released.

In recent years, there's been an increase in opportunities for other **community justice workers**. All community justice workers try to reduce and prevent crime. They may work in community safety, with victims, survivors and witnesses of crimes or with people who have offended, or who are at risk of doing so. A wide range of organisations employ community justice workers.

Getting started

- To train as a **probation officer** you take a Diploma in Probation Studies while working. The Diploma includes an NVQ in community justice at level 4 and takes about two years to complete. To train, you must have a minimum of two A levels, or equivalent, plus supporting GCSEs at grades A*-C.

- There is no one set way of entering **community justice work** – certain jobs may require specific qualifications. Experience as a volunteer is useful and can lead to paid positions. Once in work, an NVQ in community justice is available at level 3 – which can be gained through assessment in the workplace.

- You could train in work through an Advanced Apprenticeship in community justice, leading to NVQ level 3.

Find out more

Contact your local probation service; the address is in the telephone directory.

National Probation Directorate
1st Floor, Abell House, John Islip Street, London SW1P 4LH.
Tel: 020 7217 072930. www.probation.homeoffice.gov.uk
Publishes the booklet, *Careers in Probation* – available to download
from the website by following the 'join us' tab.

Skills for Justice
Centre Court, Atlas Way, Sheffield S4 7QQ.
Tel: 0114 261 1499. www.skillsforjustice.com

Youth Justice Board for England and Wales
11 Carteret Street, London SW1H 9DL.
Tel: 020 7271 3033 www.youth-justice-board.gov.uk

Working in Advice & Counselling – published by VT Lifeskills, £8.50.
Includes a profile of a probation officer.

Product design: see Art and design

Programming: see Information and communication technology

Psychology

Psychologists investigate the underlying causes of behaviour and use
this to help solve people's problems and worries.

- **Educational psychologists** usually work for local authorities.
  They advise schools, parents etc on children's emotional,
  learning and behavioural problems.

- **Clinical psychologists** are employed in the NHS helping
  people with behavioural and emotional problems, learning
  difficulties and psychological disorders. They should not be
  confused with psychiatrists, who are doctors who treat patients
  with diseases of the mind.

- **Occupational psychologists** work in government and
  industry. They may advise on recruitment and selection,
  training and how to motivate staff.

- **Counselling psychologists** help people who are having
  problems with everyday life.

- **Forensic psychologists** work with offenders and staff in prisons, special hospitals and youth custody centres.

- **Health psychologists** study people's behaviour related to health, illness and healthcare, e.g. they may help people to deal with eating disorders.

- **Sports psychologists** work with individual sportspeople and coaches to help them achieve the best possible results.

Psychologists may also work in research or teach psychology.

Getting started

- To become a chartered psychologist you need a BPS-accredited degree in psychology followed by BPS-accredited postgraduate training.

- For entry to a psychology degree course, you need at least two (usually three) A levels, or equivalent qualifications, plus supporting GCSEs at grades A*-C, usually including maths and, possibly, science subjects. A level psychology is not necessary.

Find out more

The British Psychological Society (BPS)
St Andrew's House, 48 Princess Road East, Leicester LE1 7DR.
Tel: 0116 254 9568. www.bps.org.uk
The booklet, *So you want to be a psychologist?*, is available to download from the website.

Working in Advice & Counselling (includes profiles of a clinical psychologist and occupational psychologist) and *Working in Hospitals* (includes a profile of a trainee clinical psychologist) – both published by VT Lifeskills, £8.50 each.

Pub work: see Catering and hospitality

Public health inspection: see Environmental health

Public relations

Public relations (PR) work involves establishing good relations between an organisation and its public – whether customers, shareholders or the community. It may involve dealing with the media (writing press releases, scripts, articles etc), arranging corporate hospitality, organising exhibitions and so on. PR staff have to agree what PR work is needed, plan a programme and evaluate its progress. Excellent communication, organisation and teamworking skills are required, together with creativity and stamina. PR officers may work for a large organisation with its own PR department or for a consultancy firm where they advise clients.

Getting started

- Most PR officers have a degree. This can be in any subject although there are a small number of degree and postgraduate courses in public relations which are approved by the CIPR.

- Once in employment, the CIPR offers part-time courses leading to Advanced Certificate and Diploma qualifications.

Find out more

Chartered Institute of Public Relations (CIPR)
32 St James's Square, London SW1Y 4JR.
Tel: 020 7766 3333. www.cipr.co.uk

Working in Marketing, Advertising & PR – published by VT Lifeskills, £8.50.

Publishing

Publishers select or commission articles or manuscripts from authors and arrange for their design and printing. They organise the distribution and marketing of finished books, magazines/journals and, increasingly, electronic publications, e.g. multimedia packages and CD-ROMs. There are opportunities for:

- **commissioning editors** who decide whether or not to publish a particular product – they negotiate with authors and their agents

- **production editors** who are the link between the writing team and the printer in magazine publishing

- **sub-editors** who turn material into finished articles and may write features themselves in magazines

- **copy editors** who read through text and check that it is consistent, accurate etc

- **proofreaders** who check for errors in spelling, punctuation and grammar

- **design and production staff** who turn the work into something that can be sold.

Getting started

- To work in publishing, you need to be good at English, have ICT skills and the ability to work to deadlines.

- Entry to editorial work is very competitive. It may be useful to first gain some relevant experience, e.g. in administrative or secretarial work. For magazine publishing, experience as a journalist can help. Try getting involved in editing or writing articles for your school/hobby magazine.

- There are occasional openings for those with A levels, or equivalent, but you usually need a degree. There are some in-house training schemes for graduates.

- There are a few specialist publishing degree courses or you could combine publishing with another subject, although studying publishing is not essential. For work in a specialist area, like music or scientific publishing, it is helpful to have a degree in the subject.

- If you are interested in a career in publishing, Diplomas in creative and media may be available.

Find out more

Publishers' Association
29b Montague Street, London WC1B 5BW.
Tel: 020 7691 9191. www.publishers.org.uk

Working in English (includes various profiles related to publishing) and *Working in Work Experience & Volunteering* (includes profiles on a magazine publisher and a journalist) – both published by VT Lifeskills, £8.50 each.

Purchasing and stock control

Purchasing and supply managers and officers (also known as **buyers**) work for all types of organisations. Their task is to buy materials for manufacturing goods that are to be resold and articles for use in the organisation, ranging from large items of equipment to office stationery. As supplies are often bought in bulk, purchasing staff have to have excellent negotiating and planning skills. They may also be responsible for stock control, the management of stores and the distribution of goods.

Getting started

- No specific qualifications are required for entry to purchasing and stock control. However, for in-house training schemes, most employers expect you to have at least A levels, a degree, or the equivalent.

- To enrol on the CIPS Graduate Diploma programme, you need a minimum of two A levels, or the equivalent, plus supporting GCSEs. If you have a relevant higher education qualification, you may have some exemptions. Part-time CIPS courses are run at various colleges and by distance learning.

- If you work at assistant or supervisory level, you can take the CIPS level 2 Introductory Certificate (for which there are no formal entry requirements) and the level 3 Certificate in purchasing and supply.

- NVQs are available in procurement at levels 2 to 4. These can be taken through assessment in the workplace.

Find out more

The Chartered Institute of Purchasing and Supply (CIPS)
Easton House, Easton on the Hill, Stamford, Lincolnshire PE9 3NZ.
Tel: 01780 756777. www.cips.org

Working in Retail & Customer Services, Working in Food & Drink (both include profiles of buyers) and *Working in Transport & Logistics* (includes a profile of a purchasing manager) – all titles published by VT Lifeskills, £8.50 each.

Retailing – from the *Real Life Guides* series – published by Trotman, £9.99.

Quality assurance: see Management

Quantity surveying: see Surveying

Radiography (diagnostic and therapeutic)

Radiographers usually specialise in one of two branches.

Diagnostic radiographers are responsible for producing high quality images on X-ray film, scans and other recording materials that assist in the diagnosis of diseases and the extent of injuries.

Therapeutic radiographers use radiation in the treatment of patients, often with cancer. They work closely with cancer specialists, medical physicists etc as part of the radiotherapy team.

Assistant practitioners undertake some imaging and treatment procedures on patients.

Apart from a knowledge of human physiology, radiographers have to be quite fit and strong and have good observational and people skills.

Getting started

- To practise as a **radiographer**, you have to take a degree in diagnostic or therapeutic radiography approved by the Health Professions Council. For entry, you normally need three A levels (some universities require a science subject) plus supporting GCSEs at grades A*-C, often to include maths, English and a science. A level-equivalent qualifications may be acceptable, but check whether this is the case.

- After gaining experience, you could take a specialist postgraduate qualification in an area of radiography that particularly interests you.

- To work as an **assistant practitioner**, you may need particular GCSEs; assistants can work towards NVQ level 3 in health (radiotherapy or clinical imaging).

Find out more

The Society and College of Radiographers
207 Providence Square, Mill Street, London SE1 2EW.
Tel: 020 7740 7200. www.sor.org

NHS Careers
Tel: 0845 60 60 655. www.nhscareers.nhs.uk and
www.stepintothenhs.nhs.uk
Produces a range of careers leaflets.

National Leadership and Innovation Agency for Healthcare
For information on training in Wales, click on 'Careers' on:
www.nliah.wales.nhs.uk

Health Professions Council
Park House, 184 Kennington Road, London SE11 4BU.
Tel: 020 7582 0866. www.hpc-uk.org
Website gives details of standards and approved courses.

Recreation management: see Leisure management

Reflexology: see Complementary medicine

Refrigeration: see Building services engineering

Religious work

Religious organisations, such as Baptists, Hindus, Buddhists, Jews etc recruit religious leaders who have a strong faith, maturity and commitment. There may also be opportunities in administration, secretarial work, fundraising, publicity, or work with young people etc.

In the Christian churches, ordained ministers preach the faith, conduct services, baptisms, weddings and funerals as well visiting the ill and the bereaved. There are other openings for employment, e.g. youth work, social work and missionary work for which a professional qualification may be required – although there are, in some cases, denominational training courses. In certain religions e.g. the Roman Catholic Church, only unmarried men may be ordained.

Getting started

- Religious work is a vocation – if you think you might be interested, it is useful to carry on with your education as far as possible – you could study theology, but this is not essential. Alternatively, you could undertake training in nursing, teaching or social work etc to help you develop relevant skills. Voluntary work is also useful to gain experience.

- To enter the ministry you take a course at a theological or Bible college. The length of the course and the qualifications required depend on your age and denomination. Many candidates have a degree, but this is not essential.

Find out more

Talk through your plans with religious representatives at your place of worship.

Residential care: see Social work

Retailing

Over three million people in the UK are employed in retail – in small shops, supermarkets, large department stores, in mailorder firms, in wholesalers and online shopping etc. Most have contact with the customers but buyers, merchandisers, marketing specialists, warehouse workers, finance and ICT staff and so on work behind the scenes. There are jobs in retailing for people at all levels of educational attainment, from checkout cashiers to senior managers. Sales staff need to be able to get on well with customers and, for some jobs, they need specialised knowledge of the products or services they sell.

Getting started

- Try to gain experience in retail through part-time weekend or holiday work while studying.

- **Sales staff** do not usually need many qualifications to start work – personality is at least as important. However, there are full-time A level and BTEC courses which may be helpful.

- You could train through an Apprenticeship or Advanced Apprenticeship, leading to NVQs at levels 2 and 3 respectively.

- Once in employment, NVQs in different aspects of retail work are available through assessment in the workplace.

- There are specialist qualifications offered by bodies which represent particular types of shops, e.g. florists, butchers, pet shops, jewellers and health food stores.

- There are foundation degree, HND and degree courses in **retail management**.

- Many employers offer in-house management training programmes for those with A levels (or equivalent) or degrees.

- Some 14- to 16-year-olds may have the opportunity to take a Young Apprenticeship in retailing, combining learning and work experience with an employer with study at school and college.

- If you are interested in a career in retailing, Diplomas in retail are being introduced from 2010.

Find out more

Skillsmart Retail
93 Newman Street, London W1T 3EZ.
Tel: 0800 093 5001. www.skillsmartretail.com
Contact for information on retail training and qualifications.

Working in Retail & Customer Services and *Working in Food and Drink* – both published by VT Lifeskills, £8.50 each.

Retail – from the *Real Life Guides* series – published by Trotman, £9.99.

How to Get Ahead in Retail – published by Heinemann, £12.99.

Robotics: see Engineering

Roofing work: see Building crafts

Royal Air Force

National defence is the main task of all branches of the Armed Forces. They also take part in peacekeeping operations. The RAF offers over 60 careers – in addition to flying as aircrew, there are opportunities in engineering, communications, catering, logistics, medical and dental work, and security work, to name but a few. With the exception of the RAF Regiment, all jobs are open to men and women.

As in all the Armed Forces, you have to be physically fit and pass medical tests. There are also nationality requirements. You need to be able to work in a team, have good judgement, self-discipline and accept that life in the RAF has its dangers.

Getting started

- You can usually enter the RAF as an **airman/airwoman** from the age of 16. For some trades, no formal entry qualifications are necessary, but certain aircrew, technical and medical trades specify particular GCSEs or professional qualifications. Once in the RAF, airmen/airwomen can take internal qualifications and also gain NVQs, BTEC qualifications etc.

- To enter the RAF as a **non-commissioned officer**, you need a minimum of five GCSEs at grades A*-C, including English, maths and a physics-based science. Other subjects are also specified for some branches. You must be at least 17 and six months on entry.

- To enter the RAF as a **commissioned officer**, you need at least five GCSEs at grades A*-C, including English and maths, and two A levels, or the equivalent. Entry is from the age of 17 and six months. You will be given an initial interview at the Armed Forces Careers Office (RAF). You will then attend a selection board and take aptitude tests to assess your leadership potential.

- A range of scholarship and sponsorship schemes is available through the RAF, e.g. to give you financial assistance towards the cost of A level study or a degree.

- If you are interested in joining the Armed Forces, Diplomas in public services are being introduced from 2010.

Find out more

Visit your local **Armed Forces Careers Office** (RAF) – look in the phone book under 'Royal Air Force'.

Careers information is available of the RAF careers website: www.raf.mod.uk/careers

The Armed Forces – from the *Real Life Guides* series – published by Trotman, £9.99.

How to Get Ahead in the Armed Forces – published by Heinemann, £12.99.

Royal Navy and Royal Marines

The Royal Navy is concerned with defence while the Merchant Navy transports cargo and passengers around the world (see under *Merchant Navy*). National defence is the main task of all branches of the Armed Forces. They also take part in peacekeeping operations. Within the **Royal Navy ranks**, there is a wide range of trades. The main trade categories are warfare, engineering, logistics, medical and the Fleet Air Arm. **Royal Navy officers** can specialise in warfare, engineering, training management, aviation or medical work. The **Royal Marines** are commando troops, specialising in snow, jungle, mountain and amphibious warfare. They are exceptionally tough, fit soldiers.

Mine clearance diving, submarine work and the Royal Marines (frontline combat roles) are the only areas not currently open to women. As in all the Armed Forces, you have to be physically fit and pass medical tests; you also have to pass a Royal Navy Swimming Test. There are also nationality requirements. You need to be able to work in a team, have good judgement, self-discipline and accept that life in the Royal Navy and Royal Marines has its dangers.

Getting started

- Assessment tests help you and the Navy decide which work area you are most likely to be suited to. For entry to most of the jobs in the **Royal Navy ranks** (ratings), you need to be aged 16 or over and there are usually no particular GCSE requirements. However, there are some jobs (e.g. communications technician) for which you need to have specific GCSEs at grades A*-C. The age of entry for medical assistants is from 17.

- For **Royal Navy officer** training, you can enter the Naval College with at least five GCSEs at grades A*-C (including English and maths) and 140 UCAS Tariff points. You have to be 17 or over. Alternatively, you can enter the Navy as a graduate having completed a degree acceptable to the Ministry of Defence (consult your local naval careers liaison officer for details). All officer applicants appear before the Admiralty Interview Board and also take several practical and written tests.

- The Royal Navy offers a number of sponsorship and bursary schemes for potential officers, e.g. for sixth form or university study.

- No formal entry qualifications are required for entry to the ranks in the **Royal Marines**. Entry is from the age of 16. Musicians and buglers have an audition and train at the Royal Marines School of Music. Officer entry in the Royal Marines is similar to the Royal Navy.

- Once in the Royal Navy/Royal Marines, you can work towards internal, professional and nationally-recognised qualifications, such as NVQs and HNCs.

- If you are interested in joining the Armed Forces, Diplomas in public services are being introduced from 2010.

Find out more

The Royal Navy and Royal Marines

Hotline: 0845 607 5555.

www.royalnavy.mod.uk/careers

There are 48 leaflets on different trades which can be downloaded from the website.

Visit your local **Armed Forces Careers Office** (Royal Navy and Royal Marines) – look in the phone book under 'Royal Navy'.

The Armed Forces – from the *Real Life Guides* series – published by Trotman, £9.99.

How to Get Ahead in the Armed Forces – published by Heinemann, £12.99.

Rural surveying: see Surveying

Safety work

Safety officers are employed by industrial and commercial organisations to make sure that safe and healthy systems of work are used, that accidents are reported and that the legal requirements are met. **Health and safety inspectors** are employed by the HSE. They visit factories and commercial premises to check that various health and safety laws and regulations are being obeyed. Much of the work involves informing, persuading and encouraging rather than enforcing the law. Safety officers and inspectors need the ability to communicate at all levels, confidence, patience, determination and decisiveness.

Getting started

- Most safety officers are graduates who study part-time for qualifications accredited by IOSH or for NVQs in occupational health and safety at levels 3-5.

- To be an HSE inspector, you need a degree, or equivalent qualification, or at least two years' work experience, with evidence of work-based learning and/or professional qualifications.

- New HSE inspectors undergo on- and off-the-job training for two years. You have to continually update your knowledge.

Find out more

Health and Safety Executive (HSE)
Info line: 0845 435 0055. www.hse.gov.uk

Institution of Occupational Safety and Health (IOSH)
The Grange, Highfield Drive, Wigston, Leicestershire LE18 1NN.
Tel: 0116 257 3100. www.iosh.co.uk

Scaffolding: see Building crafts

Science: see Biochemistry, Biology, Chemistry, Laboratory technician work, Physics

---

Sculpture: see Art and design

Secretarial work

Secretaries are employed in almost every organisation. Job titles vary, e.g. personal assistant, administrative assistant, secretary and clerical assistant. The degree of responsibility that a secretary is given also varies. Most secretaries need keyboard skills in order to wordprocess documents. Shorthand and audio-typing skills are still in demand despite the increase in office technology. Secretaries may write and deal with correspondence themselves, do filing, make appointments, sort the post, make travel and hotel arrangements, prepare agendas and keep minutes of meetings.

There are opportunities to specialise, e.g. in agricultural, legal, bilingual or medical secretarial work. Secretaries need good organisational skills and must be able to pay attention to detail.

Getting started

- It is possible to enter secretarial work with limited responsibility with GCSEs and some keyboard skills. However, you should aim to get at least some GCSEs (or equivalent) at grades A*-C, including English, and preferably, maths. Subjects such as languages, business and ICT are also useful. An AS/A level in business studies or applied business, or an appropriate OCR or BTEC National qualification would give you a wider knowledge of the business world and may lead to a job with more responsibility.

- NVQs in business and administration are available at levels 1 to 4. These may be gained through assessment in the workplace and/or study at a college or training centre.

- Apprenticeships and Advanced Apprenticeships in business administration are available which offer training in the workplace leading to NVQs.

- You could take a full- or part-time secretarial course at a further education or private college. Qualifications are offered by bodies such as Pitman, OCR and the LCCIEB and there are colleges' own awards. Entry requirements vary. Some college courses allow you to specialise, e.g. in medical secretarial work.

- It's possible to take a degree and then a secretarial course designed for graduates.

- Some 14- to 16-year-olds may have the opportunity to take a Young Apprenticeship in business administration, combining learning and work experience with an employer with study at school and college.

- If you are interested in a career in secretarial work, Diplomas in business, administration and finance are being introduced from 2009.

Find out more

Institute of Qualified Private Secretaries Ltd

Suite 464, 24-28 St Leonards Road, Windsor, Berkshire SL4 3BB.
Tel: 0844 8000 182. www.iqps.org

Working in English – published by VT Lifeskills, £8.50. Includes a profile of a personal assistant.

Security work: see Police and security services

Shiatsu: see Complementary medicine

Shipbroking: see Logistics and transport

Shop work: see Retailing

Social work

Professional social workers support individuals and families to help them overcome difficulties in their lives, such as dealing with illness or unemployment. They may work with a particular client group, e.g. young children or older people. Local authority social services departments employ most social workers, but there are opportunities within NHS trusts, criminal justice services, charities and other organisations. Social workers need to be patient, determined, observant, open-minded and able to help people without getting personally involved.

Social work assistants help professionally-qualified social workers in their day-to-day work. They may make routine visits to assess people's needs, follow up enquiries and liaise with other agencies.

Care assistants are employed in a wide range of organisations – they may work in day centres, residential homes, nursing homes and in the community. They provide care and help with everyday things like dressing and eating.

Getting started

- To be a **professional social worker** you have to take an approved social work degree. The degree usually takes three years, full time but other routes are also available, e.g. for graduates and those already working in the area. For the degree course you need at least two A levels, or equivalent, plus GCSE English and maths at grades A*-C (or equivalent).

- There are no specific entry qualifications for **social work assistants**, however, employers usually look for a good standard of education and experience working with people. You train mainly through in-service courses.

- No formal qualifications are usually required for **care assistant** posts but once in employment, you can work towards NVQs. Apprenticeships and Advanced Apprenticeships in health and social care are available which offer training in the workplace leading to NVQs.

- Courses in health and social care can be useful for caring careers. At school you may have the opportunity to take a GCSE in health and social care. Most colleges offer relevant courses, such as AS/A levels, BTECs and OCR Nationals in health and social care. Diplomas in society, health and development may also be available. If you are interested in professional social work, check whether the course you want to take is acceptable for entry to a social work degree.

- Some 14- to 16-year-olds may have the opportunity to take a Young Apprenticeship, combining learning and work experience with an employer with study at school and college.

Find out more

Careers in Social Work and *Working in Social Care* – booklets available from the Department of Health, tel: 0845 604 6404, or view:
www.socialworkandcare.co.uk/socialwork
www.socialworkandcare.co.uk/socialcare

Care – from the *Real Life Guides* series – published by Trotman, £9.99.

Working in Advice & Counselling – published by VT Lifeskills, £8.50.

Software engineering: see Information and communication technology

---

Solicitor: see Legal work

Speech and language therapy

Speech and language therapists (SLTs) help adults and children to overcome communication and swallowing problems. Trained therapists work in hospitals, schools, community clinics and clients' homes. They work closely with other professionals, such as psychologists, doctors and social workers. SLTs need good observational skills, patience, imagination and excellent communication skills.

Speech and language therapists' assistants work under the direction of qualified therapists. Their duties may include routine work with clients, preparing rooms and equipment and administrative tasks.

Getting started

- To work as a **SLT**, you must be registered with the Health Professions Council (HPC) having completed an HPC-accredited course. This is either a three- or four-year degree or a two-year postgraduate course. For a degree course you need a minimum of three A levels, preferably including biology or another science, and five GCSEs at grades A*-C, including English. Equivalent qualifications may be acceptable.

- There are no set entry qualifications to work as a **speech and language therapist's assistant**. Once in employment, you can work towards the NVQ level 3 in health and take the option in speech and language therapy.

Find out more

Royal College of Speech and Language Therapists
2 White Hart Yard, London SE1 1NX.
Tel: 020 7378 1200. www.rcslt.org
Produces a booklet, *A career in speech and language therapy*, which can be downloaded from the website.

NHS Careers
Tel: 0845 60 60 655. www.nhscareers.nhs.uk and www.stepintothenhs.nhs.uk
Produces a range of careers leaflets.

National Leadership and Innovation Agency for Healthcare
For information on training in Wales, click on 'Careers' on:
www.nliah.wales.nhs.uk

Health Professions Council
Park House, 184 Kennington Road, London SE11 4BU.
Tel: 020 7582 0866. www.hpc-uk.org
Website gives details of standards and approved courses.

Working in Community Healthcare – published by VT Lifeskills, £8.50.
Includes a profile of a speech and language therapist.

Sports and fitness instructing

Sports and fitness instructors tend to specialise in one particular sporting activity. They may take aerobics and keep-fit classes or plan exercise programmes for individuals to use in a gym. They teach sports, such as swimming, golf, tennis, squash or team games to amateurs as well as coaching professionals. Work may be full time or part time in private health clubs, colleges, local authority sports and leisure centres etc. Sports instructors need to be good motivators and to always pay attention to health and safety.

Getting started

- The national governing bodies of most sports (e.g. the Football Association) offer their own instructor qualifications. These are required for most paid jobs.

- NVQs are available in instructing exercise and fitness and also sports development.

- Some instructors are qualified as recreation managers or as physical education teachers.

- Nationally-recognised qualifications in instructing/fitness are needed at level 2 in order to become a qualified fitness instructor. This also enables you to join the Register of Exercise Professionals.

- Apprenticeships and Advanced Apprenticeships offer training leading to NVQ levels 2 and 3, in areas such as active leisure and learning.

- Some 14- to 16-year-olds may have the opportunity to take a Young Apprenticeship combining learning and work experience with an employer with study at school and college.

- If you are interested in a career in sports and fitness instructing, Diplomas in sport and leisure are being introduced from 2010.

Find out more

CCPR
Burwood House, 14-16 Caxton Street, London SW1H 0QT.
Tel: 020 7976 3900. www.ccpr.org.uk

SkillsActive
Castlewood House, 77-91 New Oxford Street, London WC1A 1PX.
Careers Advice Helpline: 08000 933300 www.skillsactive.com/careers

Sport & Fitness Uncovered – published by Trotman, £11.99.

Stage management: see Drama

Statistics

Statisticians design ways to collect numerical information and data from a variety of sources so that good decisions can be made. They then analyse and interpret the data, and present their findings in the clearest possible way with graphs, charts, diagrams, tables and written reports. Much of the analysis work is done with the help of computer programs. Statisticians work in a variety of settings, including government departments, business and industry. They need a high level of mathematical ability, a logical mind and good problem-solving skills.

Getting started

- To be a professional statistician you need a degree in statistics (or in maths with statistics options). For entry to a degree course you have to have at least two (often three) A levels, or equivalent, including maths. Alternatively, you can take a first degree in maths, economics or a science followed by a postgraduate course in statistics.

- The Royal Statistical Society's professional qualifications can be taken part-time. There are three levels: Ordinary Certificate in Statistics (which requires a good grade in GCSE maths, or the equivalent, or relevant work experience); Higher Certificate; Graduate Diploma (the equivalent of an honours degree in statistics).

Find out more

Royal Statistical Society
12 Errol Street, London EC1Y 8LX.
Tel: 020 7638 8998. www.rss.org.uk

Careers with a Science Degree – published by Lifetime Publishing, £11.99.

Working in Science – published by VT Lifeskills, £8.50. Includes a profile of an investigator statistician.

Steeplejacking: see Building crafts

Stock market work

The London Stock Exchange is a market place where shares are bought and sold. It is actually a collection of members of stockbroking firms. The Exchange sees that the market is working efficiently and fairly. **Stockbrokers/dealers** buy and sell stocks and shares on behalf of their clients (who may be major investors or private individuals) and help them to manage their investments in order to get the best financial returns. **Market makers** buy stocks and shares in a speculative way with the aim of selling them at a profit. All Stock Exchange staff have to keep up to date with what is happening in business and in the stock market. They also have to be able to work under pressure.

Getting started

- Although there are no formal entry requirements for working as a stockbroker/dealer or market maker, in practice, you probably need a degree. A background in economics, finance or business is useful, but any degree is acceptable.

- Training is mainly on the job. In order to give investment advice and/or to trade, you must be 'approved' by the Financial Services Authority. This involves achieving certain qualifications, such as those offered by the Securities Institute.

Find out more

London Stock Exchange Ltd
10 Paternoster Square, London EC4M 7LS.
Tel: 020 7797 1000. www.londonstockexchange.com

Financial Services Skills Council
51 Gresham Street, London EC2V 7HQ.
Tel: 0845 257 3772. www.fssc.org.uk

Stone masonry: see Building crafts

Surgery: see Medicine and surgery

Surveying

Surveying is the measurement, valuation, management and development of all kinds of buildings and land. There are various branches of surveying and just some are described here. Surveyors must be practical, have good problem-solving and analytical skills.

- **Building surveyors** inspect buildings and make reports on their structural condition. They can advise clients on the suitability of a building for specific purposes, prepare schemes for conversion or repair and advise on costs.

- **Quantity surveyors** work out the costing of a building project and are employed in large building contractors and civil engineering firms, in local and central government departments and in private practice, such as in specialist firms of quantity surveying consultants.

- **Rural surveyors** value land, farm machinery, timber etc and advise on the use and development of agricultural land.

- **Land surveyors** measure the land and all the physical features so that maps/plans can be prepared. Many land surveyors work abroad. See also *Cartography*.

Technical surveyors work alongside chartered surveyors in all branches. They provide assistance, support and specialist knowledge. There are also professionally-qualified surveyors who do not have chartered status.

See also *Estate agency, auctioneering and valuation*.

Getting started

- To qualify as a **chartered surveyor**, you must complete a degree accredited by RICS. There are part- and full-time degrees in different branches of surveying, so the subjects you need at A level (or equivalent) vary. However, you will probably find that science, maths and technology subjects are appropriate. If you have a relevant foundation degree or HNC/D, you may be able to enter the second year of a degree course. If you have a degree in another subject, you can take an accredited postgraduate qualification. Once you have your degree or postgraduate diploma, you must complete at least two years of structured training in employment before undertaking the RICS assessment for chartered status.

- To enter work at a lower level as a **technical surveyor**, you would need at least an appropriate BTEC National course or similar qualification. Four GCSEs at grades A*-C (or the equivalent) are usually required, to include maths, English and, possibly, science. You can then take a relevant HNC/D, or an NVQ level 4, followed by a period of training in employment and a RICS assessment. You could enter employment with a relevant HNC/D at a higher level. It is possible to progress from a technical surveyor to chartered surveyor.

- There are a number of professional bodies related to surveying (apart from RICS), each with their own qualification requirements for entry. Which you choose may depend on which branch of surveying you intend to specialise in.

Find out more

RICS

Surveyor Court, Westwood Way, Coventry CV4 8JE.
Tel: 0870 333 1600. www.rics.org.uk

Working in the Built Environment & Construction – published by VT Lifeskills, £8.50. Includes profiles of various surveyors.

Construction – from the *Real Life Guides* series – published by Trotman, £9.99.

Systems analysis: see Information and communication technology

Teaching

Teachers work with children, young people and adults in a variety of settings (schools, sixth form colleges, nurseries, prisons, adult education centres, further education colleges etc). They help students to learn through developing their understanding and creative thinking. Primary teachers cover all subjects in the primary curriculum while secondary teachers are subject specialists. Teachers need dedication, commitment, imagination, good organisation and communication skills.

Teaching assistants support qualified teachers and individual pupils.

Getting started

- To qualify to teach in schools, you need to follow approved training which leads to **Qualified Teacher Status** (QTS). In England, in order to gain QTS, you have to pass tests in literacy, numeracy and ICT. All applicants to teacher training are expected to have GCSEs at grades A*-C in English and maths (or equivalent). For teaching younger children, e.g. in primary school, you also need to have GCSE at grade A*-C in a science subject.

- You could take a Bachelor of Education (BEd) degree course with QTS. Some institutions offer QTS with a Bachelor of Arts (BA) or Bachelor of Science (BSc) degree course. The degree route is most suitable if you want to teach in nursery, junior or the lower years of secondary school. Your advanced-level subjects should normally be relevant to the subject you wish to specialise in teaching.

- Alternatively, you could take a degree in an appropriate subject and then a one-year Postgraduate Certificate in Education or Professional Graduate Certificate in Education (PGCE). This route is most suitable if you want to teach in senior schools.

- There are also employment-based routes leading to QTS.

- Once you qualify as a teacher, you have to successfully complete an induction period.

- If you want to teach in further education, there are specific qualifications.

- You could take a course in teaching which follows a particular approach, such as Montessori education – however, these types of courses do not usually qualify you to teach in state schools.

- **Teaching assistants** may have the opportunity to work towards a number of different qualifications – from NVQs to foundation degrees.

Find out more

The Training and Development Agency for Schools
151 Buckingham Palace Road, London SW1W 9SZ.
Teaching Information Line: 0845 6000 991. For Welsh speakers: 0845 6000 992. www.tda.gov.uk

Working in Schools & Colleges and *Working in English* (includes profiles of people working in education) – both published by VT Lifeskills, £8.50 each.

Teaching Uncovered – published by Trotman, £11.99.

Television work: see Media: radio, TV, film and video/DVD

Textile technology

Textile technologists apply their scientific knowledge to the manufacture and use of fibre, yarns and fabrics for the production of clothing, furnishings and carpets. They research and develop new products, supervise the commissioning and installation of machinery, and make decisions about the many highly-technical processes involved in spinning, weaving, dyeing and finishing.

Textile technicians are involved in the maintenance and repair of textile machinery, quality control and the various production processes. Technicians have to solve problems in complex machines quickly to avoid delays in production. Many technicians have skills in mechanics and electronics.

Craft-level workers maintain the day-to-day running of textile machinery and **production workers** operate the machines themselves.

Getting started

- For production and **craft-level work**, you may not need specific qualifications for entry to training, but you must be good with your hands and a quick and accurate worker.

- To work as an apprentice **textile technician**, you may need four GCSEs at grades A*-C, usually including maths, a science and English.

- Some factories using highly automated systems employ graduates in disciplines such as electrical engineering.

- Once in the workplace, NVQ at levels 1-3 are available in manufacturing textiles. Apprenticeships are available which offer training in the workplace, leading to NVQs. These are suitable if you are interested in technician- or craft-level work.

- If you want to continue with your studies, you can follow a full or part-time college course, e.g. for a BTEC National or Higher National qualification in textiles.

- To work as a **textile technologist**, you normally need a degree in a subject related to textile technology. Science GCSEs and A levels, or equivalent qualifications, may be required for entry. Alternatively, you could take a science or engineering degree and then a postgraduate qualification.

Find out more

The Textile Institute
1st Floor, St James's Buildings, Oxford Street, Manchester M1 6FQ.
Tel: 0161 237 1188. www.texileinstitute.org
See website for information about professional qualifications and accredited courses.

Skillfast-UK
www.skillfast-uk.org
For information on career opportunities in the technical aspects of textiles, see: www.futuretextiles.co.uk

Working in Fashion & Clothing – published by VT Lifeskills, £8.50. Includes a profile of a senior garment technologist.

Therapeutic horticulture: see Creative therapies

Tiling: see Building crafts

Tourism: see Travel and tourism work

Town planning: see Planning

Trading standards

Trading standards officers (TSOs) enforce the wide range of legislation promoting and protecting fair and safe trading practices. They also advise members of the public and business people on trading issues, and may get involved in a much wider range of duties, such as taking samples of goods for analysis, checking weighing equipment, investigating fraudulent trading and enforcing animal health laws. TSOs must be tactful, firm and impartial. They have to have excellent powers of observation and good problem-solving and communication skills.

Enforcement officers support TSOs and **consumer advisers** deal with the public answering queries about unsatisfactory goods. They may also do administrative work and can pass on cases to TSOs for further investigation.

Getting started

- There are a number of ways to train as a **TSO**.

- You could take professional qualifications in consumer affairs and trading standards offered through the Trading Standards Institute (TSI); most people take these through distance learning. There are four levels: the Foundation Certificate, Module Certificate, Diploma and Higher Diploma. These qualifications are gained through a mixture of exams and assessments.

- Graduates with a degree accredited by the TSI can go straight into Higher Diploma level. Requirements for entry to degree courses vary – you usually need a minimum of two A levels, plus supporting GCSEs, or equivalent, including maths, English and a science. It takes up to a year to gain the necessary skills after gaining a degree.

- Another way to train as a TSO is to take a degree in any subject, followed by an accredited, one-year, full-time conversion course, followed by work experience.

- Alternatively, you can work your way up through the qualifications framework by studying while in employment in a supporting role.

- For entry to **consumer advisory work**, you may need five GCSEs at grades A*-C, but requirements vary depending on the employing authority. It's important to have good communication skills.

Find out more

Trading Standards Institute (TSI)
First Floor, 1 Sylvan Court, Sylvan Way, Southfields Business Park, Basildon, Essex SS15 6TH.
Tel: 0870 872 9000. www.tscareers.org.uk

Local government careers information can be found on: www.LGcareers.com

Working in Retail & Customer Services – published by VT Lifeskills, £8.50. Includes a profile of a trading standards officer.

Translation: see Language work

Transport and logistics: see Logistics and transport

Travel and tourism work

Tour operators put together packages to make up holidays. They arrange airline, ferry and coach seats, hotel rooms, meal plans and holiday activities. They also develop new ideas for package holidays and produce brochures. The holidays are usually sold to the public through travel agencies. Small tour operators, especially those putting together special interest or adventure holidays, may sell directly to the public.

Travel agents act as a link between the client and the tour operator. They arrange holidays and business travel. They sell air, ferry, coach and train tickets, make hotel bookings and sell package holidays arranged by the tour operators. Besides arranging travel, agents may also organise insurance, issue foreign currency, advise on visas, passports and so on.

Getting started

- Although there are no set entry requirements to work in travel and tourism, some employers ask for a few GCSEs at grades A*-C, or equivalent. Useful GCSE subjects include maths, English, a modern foreign language, geography, ICT and leisure and tourism. Many entrants offer higher-level qualifications.

- Diplomas in travel and tourism will be available in some schools and colleges from 2010.

- Once in employment, you can work towards an NVQ at level 2 or 3 in a relevant aspect of travel services.

- You could train in the workplace through an Apprenticeship or Advanced Apprenticeship leading to NVQs at levels 2 and 3 respectively.

- If you want to continue studying, you could take a specialist full- or part-time course, e.g. an AS/A level or a BTEC First or National in travel and tourism. Alternatively, there are business courses with travel and tourism options.

- If you are aiming at a job with more responsibility, such as in travel and tourism management, there are appropriate degree, HND and foundation degree courses. It's also possible to take a degree in any subject and follow it with a postgraduate course in tourism.

- Tour operators and travel agents must be able to work accurately, even when under pressure. It helps to have an outgoing, confident personality and to have a real interest in travel.

Find out more

Institute of Travel and Tourism
PO Box 217, Ware, Hertfordshire SG12 8WY.
Tel: 0844 4995 653. www.itt.co.uk

People 1st

2nd Floor, Armstrong House, 38 Market Square, Uxbridge UB8 1LH.
Tel: 0870 060 2550. www.people1st.co.uk

Travel Industry Uncovered – published by Trotman, £11.99.

Travel & Tourism – from the *Real Life Guides Series* – published by Trotman, £9.99.

Working in Cultural Heritage – published by VT Lifeskills, £8.50. Includes profiles of a tourist information centre assistant and a boat guide.

Underwriting: see Insurance

Valuation: see Estate agency, auctioneering and valuation

Vehicle engineering: see Motor vehicle work

Veterinary work

Veterinary surgeons, usually known as 'vets', diagnose diseases/injuries and treat animals (pets or farm animals) by medicine and surgery. They advise on animal health and welfare, and on breeding. Vets may work in general practice, in industry, for animal welfare charities, research institutes or for zoos and wildlife parks.

Veterinary nurses help veterinary surgeons. They have a wide range of duties, including feeding, cleaning and exercising animals; preparing equipment for operations; performing minor surgery under the direction of the vet; keeping records of progress and running tests on urine, blood etc.

Getting started

- To enter veterinary training, you need to gain relevant experience working with animals.

- To practise as a **vet**, you must be registered as a member of the Royal College of Veterinary Surgeons (RCVS). To do this, you need an RCVS-approved degree in veterinary science or veterinary medicine. Excellent grades both at GCSE (or the equivalent) and at A level are required for degree course entry.

Particular grades at GCSE in science, English and maths may be specified. Chemistry A level is normally required and several universities ask for biology. Physics or maths A level may also be specified and a non-science A level may be acceptable. A level-equivalent qualifications may be considered on an individual basis. You may be asked to take the BioMedical Admissions Test.

- To train as a **veterinary nurse** you need at least five GCSEs at grades A*-C (or equivalent), including English, maths and a science. You have to be aged 17 or over and employed full time in an RCVS-approved training practice. The training leads to NVQ levels 2 and 3 in veterinary nursing and the RCVS Certificate in Veterinary Nursing. Training takes at least two years, full time.

- It is possible to enter veterinary nurse training through an Apprenticeship.

- An alternative route is to take an RCVS-approved degree or foundation degree in veterinary nursing.

Find out more

Royal College of Veterinary Surgeons (RCVS)
Belgravia House, 62-64 Horseferry Road, London SW1P 2AF.
Tel: 020 7222 2001. www.rcvs.org.uk

The British Veterinary Nursing Association
82 Greenway Business Centre, Harlow, Essex CM19 5QE.
Tel: 01279 408644. www.bvna.org.uk

Working with Animals & Wildlife – from the *Real Life Guides* series – published by Trotman, £9.99.

Warehouse work: see Logistics and transport

Wastes management

Controlling and disposing of domestic and industrial waste is a technical and complex process. Wastes managers oversee waste operations and waste planning and offer advice. They must deal with the problems of wastes storage and transport and comply with legal regulations. Wastes managers may be employed in waste collection, waste disposal, recycling or waste regulation; there are opportunities in the public and private sectors. They need to know something about chemistry, civil engineering, geology and economics.

Getting started

- There are a number of part-time and distance-learning courses which you can take whilst in employment. For instance, there are vocationally-related qualifications at levels 3 and 4 designed the Chartered Institution of Wastes Management and the Department for Environment, Food and Rural Affairs.

- There are NVQs from levels 1 to 4 in all aspects of the wastes management industry. These involve assessment in the workplace.

- There are a number of full-time degree and foundation degree courses which include the study of wastes management. Alternatively, you could take a degree in a related subject such as environmental science, chemistry, geology, civil engineering or even business or management and then either gain direct entry into wastes management or take a relevant postgraduate qualification.

- If you manage a site which requires a wastes management licence, by law you have to hold a Certificate of Technical Competence.

Find out more

Chartered Institution of Wastes Management

9 Saxon Court, St Peter's Gardens, Marefair, Northampton NN1 1SX. Tel: 01604 620426. www.ciwm.co.uk

Working in the Environment – published by VT Lifeskills, £8.50. Includes profiles of a waste education officer and a recycling operative.

Website design: see Information and communication technology

Wholesaling: see Retailing

Wordprocessing: see Secretarial work, Information and communication technology

Youth and community work

Youth workers help young people to develop both as individuals and as members of society. Most youth workers are employed by local authorities (children's services) or voluntary organisations, such as the YMCA. Many youth workers are based in youth clubs/centres. Their work can include organising activities, counselling young people, managing the club's finances, recruiting and training volunteers and liaising with welfare groups. Youth workers may also be employed in leisure centres, in social services departments or in the community as 'detached' youth workers.

There are opportunities for **personal advisers** in the Connexions service in England. They offer a 'joined up' service for young people and need an understanding of all the different agencies which can help and advise. See also *Careers work*.

Getting started

- **Voluntary/unqualified youth workers** are given induction and basic training within the youth organisation itself.

- You may be able to get started through an Apprenticeship or Advanced Apprenticeship.

- Many unqualified youth workers take courses part time whilst working on a voluntary or paid basis. Qualifications, such as NVQs in youth work at levels 2 and 3 are available, which you can gain through assessment in the workplace. **Support staff** can build up skills and experience to help them gain entry to a higher-level course.

- To work as a **professional youth worker**, you must hold a qualification approved by the National Youth Agency (NYA) – at least a foundation degree/diploma of higher education (DipHE) in a youth and community work subject. (From 2010, you will need an honours degree.) The NYA recognises several training routes.

- Recognised DipHE, foundation degree and degree courses are available on a full- and part-time basis or through distance learning. Many DipHE and foundation degree courses offer the option of a further year of study to gain a full degree.

- It's possible to take a degree in any subject and then a recognised postgraduate course.

- For entry to higher education courses, you usually need to have at least a year's paid or unpaid youth work experience.

Find out more

National Youth Agency (NYA)
Eastgate House, 19-23 Humberstone Road, Leicester LE1 3GJ.
Tel: 0116 242 7350. www.nya.org.uk

Lifelong Learning UK
5th Floor, St Andrew's House, 18-20 St Andrew Street, London EC4A 3AY.
Tel: 0870 757 7890. www.lluk.org.uk

Working with Young People – from the *Real Life Guides* series – published by Trotman, £9.99.

Working in Advice & Counselling – published by VT Lifeskills, £8.50. Includes a profile of a youth worker.

Zookeeping

Zoos, safari parks, bird gardens and aquaria are open to the public. Staff have to balance the needs of the animals in their care and the responsibility they have to inform and educate the visitors.

Keepers are the main carers. They feed the animals, clean out their living quarters, watch for any problems and may even be involved in designing the animals' environment.

Zoologists may be employed as curators and on research projects. Their work may involve studying animals' reproduction and development, trying to understand animal behaviour and observing and measuring the interaction of animals with each other, with other species and with their environment.

Getting started

- Try to gain experience working with animals, possibly through voluntary work.

- Keepers need good communication skills, to be reliable and aware of health and safety; a driving licence is usually required. Zoologists need knowledge of scientific methods, ability with numbers, keen powers of observation, patience and problem-solving skills.

- For work as an **animal keeper**, it's helpful to have some good GCSEs, especially in English, maths and science. Higher-level qualifications can be an advantage.

- If you want to take a full-time course before entering the workplace, BTEC First and National and City & Guilds courses in animal care or animal management can provide a broad introduction.

- Once in employment, NVQs in animal care are available. Staff can take the NPTC Advanced National Certificate in the Management of Zoo Animals. This can lead to a foundation degree.

- To be a professional **zoologist**, you need to take a degree course in zoology or a related subject. For entry to a degree course, A level biology is usually required, and either one or two other science subjects (sometimes chemistry). You should certainly offer sciences and maths at GCSE grades A*-C. An A level in applied science or an A-level equivalent qualification, such as a relevant BTEC National, may be acceptable for degree course entry, but check individual requirements carefully.

Find out more

Zoological Society of London/Institute of Zoology
Regent's Park, London NW1 4RY.
Tel: 020 7722 3333 (for the Zoological Society), 020 7449 6610 (for the Institute). www.zsl.org and www.zoo.cam.ac.uk/ioz

Working with Animals & Wildlife – from the *Real Life Guides* series – published by Trotman, £9.99.

Careers guide index

Common abbreviations

Careers resources can baffle you with abbreviations. Here is a list of the more common ones you are likely to meet.

A level

An advanced-level GCE qualification. An A level course usually takes two years. The first year of study may lead to an AS qualification; the second year of study is known as A2.

AQA

The Assessment and Qualifications Alliance – an awarding body/exam board for academic and vocational qualifications.

AS level

An Advanced Subsidiary GCE qualification – may be taken after the first year of an A level course or as a qualification in its own right.

ASDAN

Award Scheme Development and Accreditation Network – an awarding body for qualifications in personal and social skills.

BA/BSc

Bachelor of Arts/Science – these are the initials given to the award of a degree. There are others too, such as BEng for Bachelor of Engineering and BEd for Bachelor of Education.

BTEC

Business and Technology Education Council qualifications are offered through Edexcel (see below). BTECs are offered in a wide range of vocational subjects at different levels.

C&G

City & Guilds – an awarding body for vocational qualifications.

CACHE

Council for Awards in Children's Care and Education.

CCEA

Council for the Curriculum, Examinations and Assessment – an awarding body/exam board for qualifications in Northern Ireland.

CoPE

Certificate of Personal Effectiveness – an ASDAN award, available at three levels, that recognises personal and social skills.

CRCI

Connexions Resource Centre Index. A method of classifying information in careers libraries.

CV

Curriculum Vitae – a document that outlines your qualifications, career history etc.

D&T

Design and technology.

DADA

Dance and drama award – financial assistance for students aged over 16 who want to work in performing arts.

DCELLS

Department for Children, Education, Lifelong Learning and Skills (for Wales).

DCSF

Department for Children, Schools and Families.

DIUS

Department for Innovation, Universities and Skills.

DipHE

Diploma of Higher Education – a qualification that usually takes two years, full-time. Can lead on to a degree.

DSA

Disabled Students Allowance – financial assistance for students with a disability, mental health condition or specific learning difficulty.

DWP

Department for Work and Pensions.

e2e

Entry to Employment – a flexible programme for people aged between 16 and 18, living in England, who are not engaged in education or training and who are not ready or able to start an Apprenticeship.

Edexcel

An awarding body/exam board for academic and vocational qualifications.

EMA

Education Maintenance Allowance – financial assistance to help those who need it in order to stay on in education after 16.

FdA/FdSc

Foundation degree (either arts or science based) – these work-related qualifications offer an alternative route through higher education. They take two years, full-time, or longer part-time.

FE

Further education.

FLT

Foundation Learning Tier – term for programmes below level 2 taken by learners over the age of 14 in England.

FMA

Foundation Modern Apprenticeship – a work-based learning programme for people living in Wales that leads to NVQ level 2, key skills and a technical certificate. In England this is known as an Apprenticeship.

GCE

General Certificate of Education – also known as an AS/A level.

GCSE

General Certificate of Secondary Education – these courses are available in a wide range of subjects and are usually taken at the end of year 11.

HE

Higher education.

HNC/HND

BTEC Higher National Certificate/Diploma – higher education qualifications awarded by Edexcel and available in many subjects.

IB

International Baccalaureate – a level 3 programme for students aged 16-19 leading to an internationally-recognised qualification.

IGCSE

International GCSE – qualifications originally designed for use overseas, but available at some independent schools as an alternative to GCSEs.

IT/ICT

Information technology or information and communication technology.

LA

Local authority.

LMI

Labour market information/intelligence. This includes statistics and information on how many people work in different areas of the country, in which industries, where there are skill shortages etc.

LSC

Learning and Skills Council – funds pre-19 learning in England. N.B. By 2010, the LSC's functions will pass to local authorities.

MA

Modern Apprenticeship – a work-based learning programme for people living in Wales that leads to NVQ level 3, key skills and a technical certificate. In England this is known as an Advanced Apprenticeship. MA can also stand for a Master of Arts, a postgraduate qualification!

NHS

National Health Service.

NMW

National Minimum Wage. A legal right for workers in the UK aged 16 and over (with a few exceptions) to be paid above set levels.

NQF

National Qualifications Framework – this sets out which qualifications are at similar levels.

NVQ

National Vocational Qualification – these are available in hundreds of occupational areas. They assess a person's competence to undertake a specific job.

OCR

Oxford, Cambridge and RSA (Royal Society of Arts) – an awarding body/ exam board for academic and vocational qualifications.

Ofqual

Office of the Qualifications and Examinations Regulator – regulates qualifications, exams and tests in England.

Ofsted

Office for Standards in Education, Children's Services and Skills – set standards for education and inspect schools, colleges etc. In Wales, a similar body is Estyn.

OU

Open University – a major provider of open- and distance-learning courses, mainly at higher education level.

PE

Physical education.

PGCE

Postgraduate Certificate of Education or Professional Graduate Certificate in Education.

PLP

Programme Led Pathway – a route into an Apprenticeship.

PLTS

Personal, learning and thinking skills.

PSHE

Personal, social, health and economic education.

QCA

Qualifications and Curriculum Authority – develops the National Curriculum.

SSC

Sector Skills Council – these provide information on training and qualifications in different occupational areas.

TfST

Time Off for Study or Training – gives 16- and 17-year-olds who are working and hold few qualifications the right to study for level 2 qualifications.

TU

Trade Union – an organisation made up of workers with the aim of protecting their rights in the workplace.

UCAS

Universities and Colleges Admissions Service – students apply through UCAS to enter full-time higher education.

VRQ

Vocationally-related qualification.

WJEC

Welsh Joint Education Committee – an awarding body/exam board for qualifications in Wales.

General index

More titles in the Student Helpbook Series ...

Decisions at 15/16+
Published in association with CRAC
A companion book to this one – the various options after year 11.
£11.99 ISBN: 978 1904979149

Decisions at 17/18+
Published in association with CRAC
Explores the main routes open to young people leaving school or college, including higher education, work with training and taking a gap year.
£11.99 ISBN: 978 1902876948

Jobs and Careers after A levels and equivalent advanced qualifications
Describes the various career opportunities open to anyone with A level, BTEC National or other level 3 qualifications.
£11.99 ISBN: 978 1904979210

A Year Off ... A Year On?
Published in association with UCAS
All the information and advice you need on how to make the most of your time out between a course or job.
£11.99 ISBN: 978 1902876863

CVs and Applications
For anyone who is applying for a job or college place; includes how to use the internet to market yourself.
£11.99 ISBN: 978 1904979203

Excel at Interviews
This highly successful book makes invaluable reading for students and jobhunters.
£11.99 ISBN: 978 1904979227

Student Life: a Survival Guide
Published in association with UCAS
Essential advice for students beginning, or soon to begin, university or college. *'... will help you budget and get the most out of your time...'* The Daily Mail
£11.99 ISBN: 978 1904979012

You can also visit our secure, eshop website: www.lifetime-publishing.co.uk where you can view our full range of resources, order and buy resources online.

Decisions at 13/14+

Jenny Barron, Tamsin Foxwell and Debbie Steel

WITHDRAWN FROM STOCK

Student Helpbook Series

Lifetime
Publishing

Decisions at 13/14+ – eleventh edition

Published by Lifetime Publishing, Mill House, Stallard Street, Trowbridge BA14 8HH

© Nord Anglia Lifetime Development South West Ltd, 2008

ISBN 978 1904979135

Printed and bound by Cromwell Press Ltd, Trowbridge

Cover design by Jane Norman

Illustrations by Royston Robertson

CRAC

The Career Development Organisation